PRUE'S PERFECT GUIDE
TO THE
SHOOT LUNCH

By the same author:
Prue's Country Kitchen
Prue's Perfect Guide to the Fishing Picnic

PRUE'S PERFECT GUIDE TO THE SHOOT LUNCH

Prue Coats

Illustrated by Ben Hoskyns

WHARNCLIFFE PUBLISHING LIMITED

First published in 1991 by
Wharncliffe Publishing Limited
47 Church Street
Barnsley, South Yorkshire S70 2AS

For up-to-date information on other titles produced
under the Wharncliffe Publishing imprint, please
telephone or write to:

Wharncliffe Publishing Limited
FREEPOST
47 Church Street
Barnsley
South Yorkshire
S70 2BR
Telephone no. (24 hours): (0226) 734555

ISBN 1-871647 061

A CIP catalogue record of this book is available from the British Library.

Printed in Great Britain at the Alden Press, Oxford

CONTENTS

Acknowledgements   vii
Introduction   1
Grouse Shooting — Driven Days   3
Grouse Shooting — The Walking-Up Day   13
Stalking   17
Partridge Shooting — Driven Days   20
Partridge Shooting — September and October   33
Partridge Shooting — Late Autumn   38
Pheasant Shooting — Lunch at Home   43
Pheasant Shooting — Lunch in a Shooting Hut   55
Pheasant Shooting — Lunch from a Land-Rover   64
Pheasant Shooting — The Four O'Clock Feast   72
Pheasant Shooting — Mid-Morning Snacks and Drinks   89
Wildfowling   94
Pigeon Shooting   98
Pigeon Shooting — Summer   104
Index   115

This book is dedicated, with love, to
Lucy and Piggy —
my sternest and greediest critics

ACKNOWLEDGEMENTS

I should like to thank the following for their invaluable help, advice, and ideas: Ben Hoskyns, for his drawings for the text and cover. Toby Buchan, my editor, and Tony Jackson, who between them hatched the whole plot, and encouraged me. Lucy, for her beady eye, her memory, and all her suggestions. Tania, Constance, Gladys, Jenny, Ann, Camilla, and all my kind friends who so willingly parted with their precious recipes. My grateful thanks also to the Game Conservancy; to Keith Howman, for allowing me to use extracts from *Prue's Country Kitchen* (World Pheasant Association, 1988); and to the Editors of *Shooting Times & Country Magazine* and of *Countrysport*.

Prue Coats
Dummer, 1991

Archie Coats

INTRODUCTION

Archie, my husband, always used to say that shoot lunches should be tasty and filling — no 'kickshaws' or 'fribbles'. The only exceptions were our shoot lunches at Tower Hill. The shooting only took a couple of hours, so if people had come a long way, Archie always reckoned we ought to provide them with something to remember, at least gastronomically, if there weren't as many birds as there should have been.

Except where you are going to shoot right through, say, in late December or early January, and can have a Four o'Clock Feast, time is always the governing factor for the food provider. No one wants to think of the beaters (who have done all the work) sitting shivering in wet clothes while the Guns eat in comfort in the warmth, so easily served — I was almost going to say 'fast' — food should be the order of the day. Something like a good hot filling stew or casserole followed by cheese, cake, fruit and chocolate to put in your pocket if the host taps his glass before you have had time to scoff any.

Main courses for shoot lunches seem to go in cycles. My least favourite was the Year of the Quiche, when wherever we went flabby quiche dogged our steps and sat heavily and indigestibly in the pits of our stomachs during the afternoon drives. I have nothing against quiche as a summer dish, but it somehow seems out of place on a dank day in November. Another of Archie's pet hates was fish pie. Again excellent as a supper dish, but not really down-to-earth enough for a hungry hunter — added to which most of the men I know hate bones (my daughter Lucy and Archie would even find one in a fish finger). I make no apologies for including some quite unusual recipes. When I suggested a cassoulet to a friend of mine she said 'Oh! do you think the men would like that?' I replied that if she didn't try she'd never know. People become conditioned to only expecting certain things to be on the

1

menu at a shoot lunch — well, jolt them out of their rut, I say. They'll be so hungry they'll eat it anyway and probably be surprised at how good it is, and in any case it will probably only be a foreign version of something they already know.

In the following pages I shall try and give you a few ideas for every kind of situation, from the grand shoot lunch in a mansion with a 'treasure' to help you serve it, to a draughty barn with straw bales to sit on, or a blasted heath with nowhere to sit and the sleet driving in your face and disintegrating your sandwich before you've even bitten into it. I have experienced most of the above-mentioned and on many of them have doubled as keeper, so in addition to remembering all the picnic paraphernalia, I have had to 'go and stop the hedge at the end of Gunners and remain there for the first three drives', or blank in the kale before breakfast just when I was hoping to get the picnic organised. In the end it simply meant getting up an hour or two earlier.

With any luck you won't have to do that, but it more than pays to make a list and organise everything the day before.

GROUSE SHOOTING — DRIVEN DAYS

AUGUST

Driven grouse shooting is inevitably going to involve four-wheel-drive vehicles, so you won't have any problem getting your picnic to the right spot at the right time. Generally there is some kind of a hut but, except in the rarefied circles of Middle Eastern potentates, no form of cooking facilities. The menu you devise should therefore comprise soup and something cold, but hot August weather will mean a lighter meal than will the driving rain and winds of October. The only time I have actually enjoyed quiche was in Inverness-shire, when our hostess produced a beautiful creamy confection made with chanterelles, those orange fungi which look like parasols blown inside out and which grow principally in birch woods. On the other hand, the least suitable 'afters' was provided by an hotel — pots of fruit-flavoured yoghurt. One year our friend Tom Gullick, who runs the wonderful partridge shooting in Spain, had flown over eight of his loaders to act as beaters. It was the old keeper's last season, and when Archie arrived he said 'Oh! Major, it's ma last season, and these bluidy furriners'll ruin it all'. Archie said, 'Just wait and see'. At the end of the day old Duncan Don came up and said 'Major, they're bluidy marrvelous, I wish they cud stay the whole season'. Feeding them was a nightmare, however, as they weren't used to Mother's Pride sliced bread, and olive oil and garlicky sausage were not at that time found in large quantities in Inverness.

Always remember that in Scotland the distances you have to travel to shop are great, and what fresh vegetables and salad you can get can be pretty mundane. It pays to take a supply of tins as a basis for some of your soups, or else to use the local produce — hence my recipe for Swede Soup (and I bet no one will guess what it is). Be sure to take plenty of spices, seasonings and dried herbs, as you are unlikely to find much in the way of herbs growing outside your shooting lodge. You may be lucky and find wild sorrel, as we did one year, in which case you can make sorrel soup. Don't be too proud to take a catering size of Hellman's mayonnaise, and pack your Magimix. I even took mine on a week's fishing holiday and never regretted it. Sharp knives are a must, as holiday catering (and other) people always seem to have blunt knives, and don't forget to take your favourite sharpener.

One year Archie and Tom took some grouse shooting in Galloway. What they omitted to say was that the lodge could only be approached up six miles of forestry road with innumerable padlocked gates. The last half-mile had to be done on foot. We were a party of twelve — Tom, his wife Mary, and their daughter, aged three; Archie and me, plus Lucy, aged four, and my 'daily' to act as nanny; Archie's brother; three cousins; and Rosie the cook girl. The first disaster was Frankie, our daily, who took one look at 'the heaps of dirt', as she called the hills, and said they frightened her. She also expected Lucy to be arrayed in her Sunday best at all times. There was no electricity, so we cooked by paraffin. I could not do the walking, which was over forestry ditches, because of a gammy leg, and after the first day Rosie the cook was commandeered to beat. So there are no prizes for guessing who was put in charge of catering. It certainly concentrated the mind wonderfully, for if you forgot, say, the bread, getting some entailed a round trip of twelve miles, which took an hour and a half. When it came to making lunch I went on strike, so everyone was press-ganged, and we used to have nightly 'bapping parties'. It was great fun but we were never able to afford it again, as so many grouse were shot that the owner put the rent up beyond the reach of our pockets.

THE DRIVEN DAY

For the driven day you will be catering for eight Guns plus wives or hangers-on, so you must think in terms of sixteen to twenty. You will need a minimum of four large thermos flasks which will each hold five 6-fl oz (150ml) Game Conservancy plastic glassfuls of soup; these glasses are absolutely ideal because even when full of hot soup they don't burn your hand. Of course you can use throw-away plastic or polystyrene cups, but they are non-biodegradable, and the others are really not much trouble to wash up. If you can bring yourself to spend the money, do invest in at least one of the stainless steel unbreakable variety of Aladdin vacuum flasks. In the end they almost pay for themselves. Until I was given one by a German who came pigeon shooting with us I reckon Archie broke one normal flask per month, and their other advantage is that flavours don't linger.

CHECK LIST

3 x 1.8-litre vacuum flasks
1 Aladdin stainless vacuum flask (optional)
20 plastic soup mugs
20 tumblers (plastic, glass or polystyrene)
1 large cold-box, plus freezer packs for drinks
1 insulated bag
Several lidded plastic boxes for sandwiches
Screwtop containers for sugar, salad dressing
Salt, pepper and mustard
1 corkscrew and bottle-opener
Favourite sharp knives and sharpener
1 food-processor (optional)
Electric hand beaters (optional)
1 adaptor for plugs, Scottish ones are often round-pin
Selection of seasoned salts, peppers and herbs
Packets of dried wild mushrooms
Cans of soup, sweetcorn, petits pois, spinach, assorted beans
4 jars quail's eggs in brine, expensive but useful
1 large catering size Hellman's mayonnaise
Selection of stock cubes, ham, chicken, beef, lamb, vegetable
Selection of sauces, Worcester, soy, anchovy etc.
Tubes tomato purée
1 large bottle best-quality, cold-pressed olive oil
1 bottle wine vinegar
Garlic

LUCY'S AMERICAN SWEETCORN AND CHICKEN SOUP

Lucy found this soup in a New England inn, owned by an Indonesian. It's almost the quickest soup in the world, and has already won legions of fans.

3 x 1lb 2oz/510g cans sweetcorn
1 x 6.24 oz/177g pot apple sauce
1 large onion, finely chopped
2 rashers bacon, finely chopped
2 oz/50 g butter
4 pints/2.3 litres chicken stock (or water

and 2 stock cubes)
1 teaspoon each chopped parsley and chives
(dried or fresh)
1 teaspoon curry powder
Salt and freshly ground black pepper

Serves 16-20

Cook the onion and bacon in the butter until soft but not coloured. Tip in the cans of sweetcorn, stir well and then process in blender or Magimix until smooth. Pour back into pan, add stock and seasonings, heat through and fill thermoses. It should not be too thick, just the right consistency to drink.

SWEDE SOUP

Even people who don't like swedes lap this up and ask for more.

2 lbs/900 g swede, peeled and cubed
8 oz/225 g potato, peeled and cubed
1 tablespoon demerara sugar
Water

Milk
Cream
Nutmeg
Salt and freshly ground black pepper

Serves 16-20

Put the swede and potato in a large pan, cover with water and add 1 teaspoon salt and the demerara sugar. Simmer over a moderate heat until tender. Drain. Process until really smooth. Replace in pan, stir in cream and season with more salt if necessary, plenty of ground black pepper and a very generous amount of nutmeg, freshly ground if possible. Thin down with milk until the right consistency is obtained. A variation of this soup can be made with turnips instead of swede.

FLORENTINE BEAN SOUP

The effects of this soup will hopefully be blown away by the brisk Scottish breezes!

---

1 x 15.2 oz/432 g tin red kidney beans	*1 dessertspoon dried basil*
1 x 15.2 oz/432 g tin haricot beans	*2 tablespoons best cold-pressed olive oil*
2 x 15.2 oz/432 g tins borlotti beans	*4 pints/2.3 litres stock (preferably ham, or*
2 hard-boiled eggs	*water and stock cube)*
2 cloves peeled garlic	*Salt and pepper*
1 tablespoon tomato purée	

Serves 16-20

Simmer all the cans of beans and the garlic in the stock until mushy. Process in the Magimix until thick but not too smooth. Add the chopped hard-boiled eggs, dried basil and olive oil and season well.

CHANTERELLE SOUP

People are far more aware of wild mushrooms now, and dried are a good substitute if it's not 'the season'. Take a few packets with you to add delicious riches to soups or stews. See the Check List (p.5).

---

2 lbs/900 g chanterelles or cultivated	*2 pints/1 litre milk*
mushrooms	*1 chicken stock cube*
2 finely chopped garlic cloves	*Lemon juice to taste*
2 oz/50 g finely chopped shallot or onion	*1 level tablespoon sugar*
2 tablespoons oil — sunflower or light olive	*1 dessertspoon dried tarragon*
oil	*1 heaped dessertspoon cornflour*
2 pints/1 litre water	*Salt and pepper to taste*

Serves 16-20

Wash the chanterelles or mushrooms and drain well. If using the dried kind, soak in boiling water for 10 minutes before using. Chop roughly in the Magimix. Heat the oil and cook the onion and garlic until soft, add the chanterelles and cook for a few minutes, stirring constantly. Add the water, milk, tarragon, sugar, stock cube and seasoning and simmer for 15-20 minutes. Thicken with cornflour and add lemon juice to taste.

GROUSE SOUP

A good way of using up all those carcasses after people have had their 'first grouse of the season' orgy.

6-8 cooked grouse carcasses, or more if you've got them
1 large unpeeled onion stuck with cloves
1 large onion peeled and chopped
2 unpeeled cloves garlic
2 carrots
4 rashers bacon chopped in pieces
1 tablespoon oil

1 tablespoon rowan or redcurrant jelly
1 tablespoon concentrated tomato purée
2 bay leaves and a bouquet garni
3 pints/1½ litres stock or water and a stock cube
1 bottle red wine
Salt and ground black pepper

Serves 16–20

Brown the chopped onion, carrots and bacon in the oil, add all the other ingredients and simmer, covered, for 3-4 hours or even longer, then drain into a clean pan. Blot off any fat with squares of kitchen paper and thicken with cornflour or just leave it as an unclarified consommé. Add a few drops of gravy browning if it looks anaemic. There are any number of delicious soups that you can make — oxtail, onion and potato with bacon, leek and potato, home-made tomato, chicken broth, to name but a few.

TRICK OF THE TRADE. If you are 'up the creek' and have run out of everything and the local village shop only has tinned peas, don't despair. Chop ½ lb/225g rashers of any kind of bacon. 'Sweat' them in a covered pan, whizz up 3 or 4 cans of tinned peas and add them to the bacon. Dilute with water, add a stock cube — ham or chicken. Season well with salt, pepper and sugar and you will find it quite delicious. Even the most pedestrian tinned or packet soup can be tarted up if you use your imagination.

Whatever you put in your sandwiches, baps, baguettes, **do be generous.** The Americans make marvellous sandwiches which seem to have more filling than flannel, so to speak. Another very important thing is what I call the 'crunch factor'. Unless the filling is creamy by design try and think of something to give it a more interesting texture. With pâté, for example, a sprinkle of chopped gherkin is an improvement, and you can use grated carrot, beansprouts or chopped fennel with cream cheese. You can freeze some kinds of plain meat, pâté or fish sandwiches, but I think they are best made fresh. You can make them the night before and put them in the fridge. Try and have some unusual breads and rolls in the freezer — you can get delicious French and Italian ones in Sainsbury's, Marks and Spencer, and other supermarkets.

Sandwiches are often improved if you spread the bread with flavoured butter, or if you prefer to use Flora, put the flavouring into mayonnaise.

BASIC FLAVOURED BUTTER

Put softened butter in Magimix, add flavouring and blend, or put in bowl and beat in with fork or electric beaters.

RAVIGOTE. *4 oz/100g softened butter; 1 teaspoon each chopped parsley, chives and tarragon; salt and pepper*

CURRIED BUTTER. *1 teaspoon each curry powder and mango chutney juice*

ANCHOVY BUTTER. *1 teaspoon Gentleman's Relish or anchovy essence*

TARTARE BUTTER. *1 teaspoon each finely chopped parsley, capers, gherkins, onion*

CUMBERLAND BUTTER. *1 teaspoon each made English mustard and Cumberland sauce.*

CUMBERLAND SAUCE. *Bring to the boil the contents of 1 x 8 oz/227 g pot of redcurrant jelly, 1 sherry glass of port, the juice of 1 orange and 1 lemon, a ½ teaspoon of ground ginger, and 1 teaspoon of dry mustard powder, and cook for 15 minutes. Peel the fruit, cut the rind in julienne strips, and blanch it in boiling water for 5 minutes, then strain and add to the sauce. Cool and refrigerate.*

Cock Capercaillie

10

SANDWICH FILLINGS

CHICKEN AND TONGUE. *4 oz/100g each, finely chopped and mixed with Ravigote Butter*

HAM. *Slices of ham on slices of bread generously spread with Cumberland Butter*

BEEF *with mayonnaise flavoured with finely chopped pickled walnut*

CHICKEN *mixed with finely chopped celery, walnuts, mayonnaise*

TUNA *mixed with finely chopped spring onion, hard-boiled egg and mayonnaise. (Optional: Anchovy Butter, see p.10).*

GROUSE. *4 cooked breasts chopped and processed in the Magimix until really fine, then add 4 oz/100 g butter, 1 teaspoon rowan jelly or bilberry jam, 1 pinch thyme, salt and black pepper*

GROUSE AND CHICKEN LIVER PÂTÉ

8 oz/225 g livers (as many grouse livers as you can get, and make up the quantity with chicken livers)	*1 teaspoon whisky*
	1 pinch thyme
	1 pinch nutmeg
4 oz/100 g butter	*Salt and pepper*

Sauté the livers in the butter until cooked but still pink inside. Place in the Magimix with all the other ingredients and process until smooth. Pour into pots, cool and then refrigerate for at least 24 hours to let the flavour develop. Sandwich between pieces of toast.

SMOKED TROUT PÂTÉ

8 oz/225 g boned and filleted smoked trout	*1 squeeze lemon juice*
1 oz/25 g butter	*1 good pinch dried dill*
1 tablespoon mayonnaise	*Salt and pepper*

Whizz everything together in the Magimix. Sandwich between thin slices of brown (preferably granary) bread or pumpernickel spread with Anchovy Butter (see p.10).

SMOKED SALMON PÂTÈ

8 oz/225 g smoked salmon pieces
4 oz/100 g cream cheese (crowdie or Caboc
should be found in Scotland)

Lemon juice
Plenty of dried dill
Generous amount of ground black pepper

Method as above.

GROUSE SHOOTING — THE WALKING-UP DAY

For the walking-up day you should organise lunch for eight Guns plus as many wives as feel energetic, so the numbers will usually work out at about ten or twelve. Food should be divided amongst three to four haversacks or, if you prefer, a plastic sandwich box for each person and one strong man to carry a couple of thermoses. Cans of beer or soft drinks should be dished out individually; be sure and find out the night before what everyone prefers. When shooting in Glen Lyon, the butler was always asked to provide a plentiful supply of water for Archie and me, so we were known as the 'Watery Coatses' for ever after. Food for this kind of caper should be nutritious, easily digestible and not too bulky. There's nothing worse than having a second 'repeat' of sardine all afternoon, so eschew anything too highly flavoured and don't go for things that are too salty. For hot drinks, coffee or tea are probably preferable to hot, thick soup, but a light kind of soup such as consommé is fine too.

Shortcrust pastry tends to disintegrate and flaky is foul and leathery when cold, so I cook sausages, preferably chipolata, and roll them up in thin slices of very new white bread (crusts cut off) spread with plenty of butter and mustard — though again, it's as well to find out who are mustard fans and who are not. Always try and include a sandwich with lettuce or tomato and don't forget an apple or an orange — very thirst-quenching. Pears and bananas bruise.

CHECK LIST
2 large thermos flasks
1 lidded plastic container per person
1 plastic mug or tumbler per person
1 can beer or soft drink per person
1 metal flask or plastic bottle whisky (bottles used for fresh citrus fruit juices from Sainsbury's and other supermarkets are just the job)
3 or 4 haversacks

TYPICAL MENU FOR A WALKING-UP DAY

TRICK OF THE TRADE. To fill a bap. Put in oven until just crisp. Cut hole in top, take out bready inside. Put in filling. Replace top.

MENU I (per person)

1 bap filled with scrambled egg and crumbled, crisply fried bacon
1 bap filled with cream cheese, chopped walnut and celery
2 Scotch pancakes sandwiched together with jam or jelly
1 Mars Bar or similar

TRICK OF THE TRADE. On these kinds of days it is a good idea to carry a couple of extra Mars Bars for your dog as they provide instant extra energy.

MENU II (per person)

½ baguette slit, spread thickly with mayonnaise and filled with slices of ham and Gruyère or Emmenthal cheese
1 bap filled with finely shredded lettuce, sliced tomato, tuna and a little of Archie's Dressing
1 chocolate brownie

ARCHIE'S DRESSING

1 heaped teaspoon Dijon mustard	*5 dessertspoons oil*
1 dessertspoon sugar	*Salt and pepper*
1 dessertspoon wine vinegar	

Shake/beat all together. Will keep for up to a week in fridge in a screw-top jar.

CHOCOLATE BROWNIES

2 oz/50 g bitter chocolate	*½ teaspoon baking powder*
2 oz/50 g butter	*¼ teaspoon salt*
8 oz/225 g plain flour	*3 oz/75 g walnut pieces*

Pre-heat oven to 350°F/175°C/Gas Mark 4. Break up chocolate with the butter and melt over a low heat. Whisk eggs and sugar until light and frothy and add chocolate mixture. Sift in flour, salt and baking powder, then stir in the nuts. Spread into an 8-inch (20-cm) square cake tin and bake for 35 minutes. Cool and cut into squares.

MENU III (per person)

1 bap thickly spread with chicken liver pâté and finely chopped gherkin
1 bap filled with lettuce and grated Cheddar cheese mixed with chutney or Branston Pickle to a spreading consistency
1 scone

NANNIE'S SODA SCONES

Archie's old nannie was a pretty hopeless cook, but the one thing she could do superbly was bake. Her scones were always a dream even though she never weighed anything. However, one day I managed to pin her down and we weighed everything out, and this is the result.

---

8 oz/225 g self-raising flour
½ teaspoon each bicarbonate of soda and
cream of tartar

Pinch salt
Milk to mix

Pre-heat oven to 425°F/220°C/Gas Mark 7. Mix dry ingredients to a soft dough with milk. Pat gently into a round on a floured board. Draw a knife lightly across so that you have 6 segments. Place on a floured baking sheet and bake for 12 to 15 minutes until risen and golden. Should melt in the mouth.

STALKING

Stalking is another ball-game altogether. You will need to be as unencumbered as possible and will not be able to afford the luxury of a thermos, though you may leave one in the vehicle to await your triumphant return with a beast (or otherwise). So the drinks problem will have to be solved by a flask of whisky to flavour the burn water or to warm you up with a nip after you have been lying in a peat hag. My mother told me that my grandfather used to have a swig of whisky and then get the stalker to pour a bottle down his back and into his boots! I only half believed her, but it was confirmed by an old friend the other day. I hasten to say that this was before the First World War so presumably the 'Water of Life' was pretty cheap, but even so it always seemed to me to be an awful waste.

Food will have to be really sustaining and not too bulky to go into a pocket, so one good sandwich/bap plus a bar of chocolate will be the order of the day. It will also have to be the kind of food that tastes just as good when squashed.

ARCHIE'S FAVOURITE

After the war, when he left the Army, Archie became a professional stalker. The deer on a friend's forest had become too numerous so had to be culled. As he had to 'do' for himself this was Archie's answer to breakfast and lunch as you could cook the first and make lunch from it in one go.

---

1 large bap	*2 streaky rashers fried until crisp*
1 fried egg	*1 oatcake*

Follow instructions for filling bap on p.14. Crumble up the oatcake into the bacon fat, fry for a few seconds and then mix with the bacon. Pack into the bap and then lay the egg on top. Season with salt and pepper and replace the hat. This is a really filling sandwich.

SAVOURY SAUSAGEBURGERS

---

1 large bap	*½ teaspoon made English mustard*
4 oz/100 g pork sausage meat	*1 teaspoon tomato ketchup*
1 pinch mixed herbs	*1 egg, scrambled*
½ teaspoon Worcester Sauce	*Salt and pepper*

Mix the sausage meat with the flavourings and make into a round flat cake, then grill or fry. Make two cuts in the bap but don't slice it right through. Put the sausage cake in the bottom half and the scrambled egg in the top. Press well together and wrap tightly in foil.

HUNTER'S SANDWICH

---

2 crusts from a new white thick-sliced loaf	*Mustard and horseradish (optional)*
1 piece of steak grilled medium rare	*Salt and pepper*

Lay the steak whilst still warm between the two crusts. Season to taste. Wrap in foil and place a 1 lb (450g) weight on top and leave for half an hour.

BACON AND LETTUCE

1 very thick slice white bread
3 rashers back bacon

Lettuce
Salt and pepper

Toast the bread under the grill. Cut off the crust at *one end only* then make a slit down it with a sharp knife leaving three crusts uncut. Fry the bacon lightly and push into the pocket, dribble in any fat and insert one or two pieces of crisp lettuce. Season and wrap in foil.

PARTRIDGE SHOOTING — DRIVEN DAYS

SEPTEMBER

No feast that I can suggest will compare with the story Archie used to tell about his father who, before the war, was invited to shoot in France where his host was the owner of one of the big three Champagne houses. After a magnificent lunch served in a marquee the Guns were told not to hurry as the next drive was a blank-in. They were ushered in to their butts, which were sunken, and there awaiting them was a table with a tray of liqueurs, a box of cigars and, draped on a couch, a girl from the Folies Bergères! This, I feel, is taking hospitality to an extreme.

'INDIAN SUMMER' FARE FOR HOT AUTUMN DAYS

Partridge shooting in Spain is another story. At about two o'clock, after a very early start, you are usually pretty hungry. You round a corner and there in front of you is a long table covered in a check cloth and laid with a variety of Spanish hors d'oeuvres interspersed with bottles of wine — no side plates, just delicious Spanish bread on which you spread your choice of goodies. The main course is cooked over a *pareja* or grill by the waiters and is generally chops or sausages. Twenty-two years ago, when we first went out to shoot with Tom, there were no Land-Rovers and the terrain over which we shot was very mountainous. Lunch was brought down by mule in panniers. Everything was organised by the shoot manager and the head keeper and the *pièce de résistance* was often a *paella al campo* made with partridge and rabbit with wild herbs. In those days many people were hungry, especially if the olive crop had failed — the most incredible sight I ever saw was when one of the beaters plucked a couple of magpies and roasted them over the fire!

On a hot September or October day in England you do not want to be faced with a heavy beef stew, so an adaptation of the kind of menu we have in Spain would be more suitable. There will more than likely be a shooting hut. Don't forget to bring plenty of soft drinks and beer. Transport them in a cold bag filled with ice or frozen sachets and, in case it is very dry, bring a large bowl and plastic container of water for the dogs.

Have on the table a selection of cold hors d'oeuvre/salad dishes and hand round a platter of sliced cold meat, poultry or pie. If you wish to have something hot hand round a light soup, consommé or a very slightly thickened vegetable soup.

CHECK LIST
Cutlery, china, tumblers
Salt, pepper, mustard, sugar
Bowls or mugs for soup
Vinicool or similar for transporting and keeping wine cool
Cold-box and freezer sachets
Ice in bucket or similar
Tonic and soft drinks in cold box or insulated bag
Gin, whisky, vodka, sherry — it's probably too hot for port or sloe gin
Corkscrew and bottle-opener
Sharp knife for emergencies
Tablecloth(s) and paper napkins

FENNEL, CHICKEN AND LEMON SOUP

This is a very quick and easily made soup, equally good hot or cold.

---

4 fat fennel bulbs, finely chopped	*little water*
2 shallots, finely chopped	*1 squeeze lemon juice*
2 pints (1 litre) good chicken stock or 2 pints (1 litre) water and 2 chicken stock cubes	*¼ pint/150 ml single cream or fromage frais (optional)*
	1 dessertspoon chopped fresh or dried fennel
1 oz/25 g butter	*1 teaspoon sugar*
1 level tablespoon cornflour mixed with a	*Salt and pepper*

Serves 16–20

Sauté the fennel and shallots in the butter until transparent then add enough stock to just cover. Simmer slowly until quite soft then blend until smooth. Pour back into the saucepan and bring to the boil. Add the cornflour and cook for a further 3 minutes, stirring constantly. Add the seasonings and squeeze of lemon juice then finally the cream.

CARROT AND CORIANDER SOUP

Another easy soup. You can get fresh coriander in plastic containers in Sainsbury's. If you can remember take it with you and add at the last moment as its delicate flavour disappears if put in too soon.

2 lbs/1 kg old carrots	1 vegetable stock cube
2 oz/50 g butter	6 coriander seeds, crushed
1 dessertspoon sugar	1 dessertspoon fresh chopped coriander if
1 pint/575 ml water	obtainable, or parsley
1 pint/575 ml milk	Salt and pepper

Serves 12-16

Peel the carrots and put them through the fine slicer of the Magimix. Tip them into a saucepan with the butter, sugar, crushed coriander seeds, salt and pepper. Cover tightly and cook until tender, shaking occasionally. Liquidize until very smooth then add the milk and water. Only use the stock cube if you think it needs body. Finally, stir in the chopped coriander or parsley.

GAME CONSOMMÉ

You've probably got a lot of undiscovered corpses at the bottom of your freezer so this is a good way to use them, unless you are like me and are a compulsive stock-maker and freezer.

2 pints/1 litre game stock	1 white of leek
2 carrots, peeled and sliced lengthways	1 bouquet garni
1 large onion, unpeeled and stuck with 6 cloves	1 tablespoon redcurrant jelly
	½ pint/275 ml sherry
1 celery stalk	Salt and pepper

Serves 12-16

Heat the stock and remove any fat by blotting with kitchen paper. Throw in all the ingredients and simmer for 1 hour. Remove the vegetables and bouquet garni with a slotted spoon and strain the soup through a tea towel folded over a colander. Adjust seasoning. It is quite unnecessary to go through all the palaver of clarifying as no one willl notice, or care, if it is not crystal clear when they drink it out of their picnic cup. The taste is what will matter.

PETA'S TUNA FISH SALAD

Always on the table for Tom's shooting lunches in Spain. It is extremely versatile, and you can substitute sardine and add cooked potato which makes it into a main course.

---

2 cans tuna	*1 apple, peeled and sliced (optional)*
6 hard-boiled eggs, roughly chopped	*1 lb cold cooked potatoes, diced or sliced*
1 Spanish onion, roughly chopped	*(optional)*
½ pint/275 ml mayonnaise, home-made or	*Pinch curry powder, salt and pepper*
Hellman's	

Serves 4-6

Drain the tuna and mix into the other ingredients with a fork. It should be on the sloppy side so you may have to add more mayonnaise. Serve with French bread. In Spain we have no side plates so cut our baguette in half and use that instead — yummy!

MUSHROOMS À LA GRECQUE

Another dish from Spain, except that it's made on site by the waiters from mushrooms picked by the beaters/loaders/Guns.

---

1 lb/450g extra small button mushrooms	*2 cloves garlic, finely chopped*
2 tablespoons extra virgin olive oil	*1 dessertspoon chopped parsley*
1 tablespoon lemon juice	*Salt and pepper*

Serves 2-4

Cook the garlic in the oil for 5 minutes, then add the mushrooms and lemon juice, salt and pepper. Simmer, covered, for another 5 minutes. Fish out the mushrooms. Reduce the liquor until it looks thick and syrupy then pour over the mushrooms. Sprinkle over the parsley and leave to cool.

TOMATO AND BASIL SALAD

1 lb/450 g tomatoes	6 basil leaves roughly torn
3 tablespoons best olive oil	Salt and freshly ground black pepper
1 dessertspoon wine vinegar	

Serves 2-4

Slice the tomatoes and lay in a shallow dish. Sprinkle over the sugar, salt and pepper and then pour over the olive oil and vinegar. Garnish with the basil leaves.

SPANISH OMELETTE

Lucy and I always quarrel over this but I suppose her method is correct as she spent a whole season working for Tom (her godfather) when she left school. Her preceptor was Alfonso the Spanish chef.

6 eggs	Oil
8 oz/225 g peeled and diced potato	Salt and pepper
8 oz/225 g peeled, chopped onion	

Serves 4-6

If you are catering for a large number of people it is best to make two omelettes — 6 eggs is about all you'll manage as you have to turn the omelette *half-way through cooking*. Heat some olive oil in a thick frying pan then put in the potato and onion. Stir briskly, lower heat and cover. Stir occasionally to prevent sticking — they should not brown. Beat the eggs with the salt and pepper then add the cooked potato and onion when slightly cool. Wipe pan clean and put in fresh oil and when smoking pour in the mixture. Lower heat and stir with a fork once or twice. When it begins to look cooked underneath slide onto a plate with the help of a spatula. Invert the frying pan over the plate and turn the pan right side up. Continue cooking until set. It should still be a bit runny in the middle. If you feel cowardly pop the pan under grill instead of going through your flipping act — not so good though. 'Oh! yes it is', Lucy says. I leave it to you to decide. Cool and cut in wedges.

SIMPLE SALADE NICOISE

Another dish you can use as a main course — just double or treble the ingredients.

2 cans tuna in oil or escabeche sauce	½ head radiccio
1 can anchovy fillets, coarsely chopped	½ head of frisée or lollo rosso
2 hard-boiled eggs, coarsely chopped	3 tablespoons cold-pressed olive oil
8 oz/225 g cold cooked potato (Pink Fir	1 dessertspoon wine vinegar
Apple, Charlotte or Belle de Fontenay	1 clove garlic
salad potatoes if possible)	1 teaspoon mild Dijon mustard
4 oz/100 g ripe black olives	1 teaspoon sugar
1 Little Gem lettuce	Salt and pepper

Serves 4–6

Mix the salad dressing (see Archie's Dressing p. 15) ahead of time in a screw-top jar and add the clove of garlic which you have slightly crushed. Shake well and leave. Mix the salad and at the last minute pour over the dressing, minus the garlic

CHICKEN SALAD

If this sounds complicated it's worth the trouble and can be made up to two days in advance and refrigerated.

1 lb/450 g cooked, diced chicken	salad potato (see above)
1 lb/450 g cooked diced ham	1 stick celery or 1 head fennel, chopped
2 lbs/900 g cooked, sliced	spring onions to garnish

Serves 10–12

To make the salad, pour your chosen sauce — home-made or Hellman's mayonnaise or Cooked Salad Dressing (see below) — over everything and mix thoroughly. Garnish with spring onions, watercress and strips of tomato or red pepper.

COOKED SALAD DRESSING

½ cup concentrated chicken stock or tinned	*1 teaspoon salt*
consommé	*¼ teaspoon pepper*
¼ cup wine vinegar	*Pinch cayenne*
5 egg yolks slightly beaten	*½ cup thick cream*
2 tablespoons made English mustard	*⅓ cup melted butter*

Put everything except the cream and butter into a bowl over a pan of hot water. Cook until it begins to thicken, stirring constantly. Add the cream and butter and cool.

BAKED SMOKED PORK LOIN WITH CHUTNEY SAUCE

Unfortunately you can't buy a whole loin very easily; the main supermarkets only go up to about 2 lbs (900g), so you will have to use two.

2 smoked pork loins	*Orange sauce (optional)*
½ cup demerara sugar	*1 tablespoon dry mustard*
½ cup peach (or mango) chutney	*1 pinch powdered cloves*
A dash of Lea & Perrins Ginger and	*Pepper*

Serves 12-16

Pre-heat the oven to 350°F/175°C/Gas Mark 4. Place the two loins in a roasting pan and cover with the rest of the ingredients which you have mixed together. Cook for 30 minutes to the lb (450 g) plus 30 minutes. Remove from pan and cool. Add a little boiling water to the roasting pan and scrape off all the brown bits. Pour into a bowl and when cool take off any fat. Slice the ham and lay down the middle of a dish. Dribble the extra sauce down the centre. Serve with wedges of Potato Galette.

POTATO GALETTE

With the addition of chopped ham, cheese, hard-boiled egg or what you will, this makes an inexpensive main course, but increase the quantities.

2 lb/900 g peeled potato (Desirée, Maris Piper or King Edward)
4 lightly beaten eggs
4 fl oz/100 ml cold-pressed olive oil
2 tablespoons chopped fresh thyme or 1

tablespoon dried
1 tablespoon chopped parsley
2 cloves garlic peeled and finely chopped
Salt and ground black pepper

Serves 8–10

Pre-heat the oven to 450°F/230°C/Mark 8. Oil a cake tin. Cook the potatoes and when done drain. Place a folded tea towel on top, and then the lid. Leave for 5 minutes. Mash thoroughly then stir in the oil and the rest of the ingredients. Tip into the cake tin and smooth down. Cook in the oven for 30 minutes until brown, then place over a high heat on top of the stove for a short time so that the sides and bottom are crisp, but be careful it doesn't burn. Cut in wedges and lift out with a cake slice or spatula. It goes very well with the ham and a crisp green salad.

PORK GALANTINE

1½ lbs/675 g minced pork
1 lb/450 g ham cut in thin strips
2 onions, finely chopped
1 oz/25g butter
4oz/ 100 g pistachio or pine nuts
6-8 rashers streaky bacon

1 teaspoon mixed herbs
½ teaspoon mixed spice
1 small glass sherry
2 bay leaves
Salt and ground black pepper

Serves 10–12

Cook the onions in the butter until soft and transparent then mix with the pork, sherry and seasonings. Line a dish with the streaky rashers, leaving 2 for the top. Fill the terrine with alternate layers of mixture and strips of ham, ending up with a layer of mince. Lay on the

2 rashers of bacon and decorate with the bay leaves. Cover tightly with foil and a lid and cook in a bain-marie in a pre-heated oven at 350°F/175°C/Gas Mark 4 for 1½ hours. Place a weight on top and when cool refrigerate for at least two days for the flavours to permeate.

VEAL PÂTÉ EN CROÛTE

This recipe was sent to me by a French friend. It would also be excellent for a grouse shooting lunch.

2 lbs/1 kg veal, minced (pork will do as a substitute)	1 dessertspoon finely chopped parsley
¾ lb/350 g ham, coarsely chopped	1 teaspoon Herbes de Provence
2-3 eggs	1 teaspoon salt
2 oz/50 g butter	½ teaspoon freshly ground black pepper
½ nutmeg, grated	1 packet puff pastry

Serves 12-16

Mix all the pâté ingredients together. Heat a little oil in a small saucepan and fry a teaspoon of the mixture. Taste to see if the seasoning is right. Adjust if necessary. Butter a roasting dish, form the mince into a long roll, dot with butter and cook in a pre-heated oven at 400°F/200°C/Gas Mark 6 for 40 minutes. Remove and allow to get quite cold. Roll out the pastry, place the 'sausage' on it. Fold one end over and seal with water. It should look like an outsize sausage roll. Brush with egg yolk and cook in a pre-heated oven at 425°F/220°C/Gas Mark 7 for 20 minutes and at 350°F/175°C/Gas Mark 4 for a further 35 minutes. Serve just warm or completely cold with watercress salad.

PORK AND APPLE PIE

This makes a nice change from the slabs of bought pork pie so often encountered at unimaginative shoot lunches.

---

3 lbs/1½ kg fillet of pork	*2 crushed cloves*
2 lbs/1 kg peeled and cored apple	*¼ teaspoon powdered bay leaves*
1 glass white wine	*¼ teaspoon ground nutmeg*
2 oz/50 g butter	*1 teaspoon chopped dried basil*
1 level teaspoon mild paprika	*Salt and ground black pepper*
Shortcrust Pastry	*5 oz/150 g butter*
10 oz/300 g flour	*3 tablespoons cold water*

Serves 12-16

Cut the fillet into thin slices. Place in a layer in the bottom of a pie dish, then a layer of apple. Sprinkle over the seasonings, pour in the wine and dot with the butter. Cover with pastry and cook at 400°F/200°C/Gas Mark 6 for 1¼ to 1½ hours. Eat hot or cold. Serve with a crisp salad of chopped celery, walnuts and raisins sprinkled with olive oil, lemon juice, salt and pepper to offset the richness of the pie.

You can allow yourself the luxury of producing a pudding at this time of the year, or if the weather is really hot a big bowl of mixed fresh fruit and a selection of light, creamy cheeses. Leave the ripe Stilton and mature Cheddar for later in the year.

TRICK OF THE TRADE. If you are taking French bread, hot it up just before you leave and wrap in foil, then newspaper, and finally some of the bubble packaging that shops use to wrap fragile objects in. Another excellent TOTT is to use polystyrene wine cases. Break French sticks in half or use half-baguettes, heat and wrap in foil and lay in the wine bottle cavities. Polystyrene fish boxes from your fishmonger are good too, provided they don't smell fishy.

SUMMER PUDDING WITH A DIFFERENCE

This is for those of you who have been filling up their Rumpot; if you haven't, just use plain fruit.

2 lbs/900 g blackcurrants, redcurrants, raspberries, strawberries	from Rumpot (optional)
	caster sugar
1 soup ladle of fruit and juice	Slices white bread, crusts removed

Serves 8-10

Any summer fruits can be used; try and include a few elderberries if you can. Cut the bread slices in wedge shapes and line a 2-pint/1-litre pudding basin. Cook the fruit gently with sugar to taste for a minute or two, add the Rumpot fruit and spoon into the basin. Top with more bread slices, carefully pour over as much juice as it will absorb and place a plate on top which will just fit inside the basin. Weight and leave overnight in fridge.
TRICK OF THE TRADE. For ease of transport leave in basin and serve direct from dish.

SOPHIE'S CHOCOLATE CAKE

My father and mother had a Polish count as farm manager just after the war. The family had escaped from Europe with hair-raising adventures and the count's mother gave me this recipe, which makes a marvellous pudding.

5 oz/150 g plain flour	3 eggs, well beaten
1 teaspoon each baking powder and bicarbonate of soda	Filling
2 tablespoons cocoa	Raspberry jam
5 oz/150 g margarine	Topping
4 oz/100 g sugar	Single cream, granulated sugar, cocoa

Serves 6-8

Cream together margarine and sugar until light and fluffy, beat in the eggs, sift in the flour, baking powder, bicarbonate of soda and cocoa. Spread evenly over a greased 10-in/20-cm tin (preferably non-stick) and cook in a pre-heated oven at 350°F/175°C/Gas Mark 4 for 20-25 minutes. Leave for a few minutes then turn out. Cut in half and spread thickly with raspberry jam while still warm. Sandwich together. When quite cool make a thick spreading mixture of cocoa, cream and granulated sugar, cover top and refrigerate.

MAGPIE

BH
1990

PARTRIDGE SHOOTING — SEPTEMBER AND OCTOBER

In early October the weather may be a bit cooler and your menu can include a light, hot main course and, as the evenings will still be pretty light, you can still go the whole hog and include a pudding. Driven partridge shooting is a relatively relaxed affair and the host may delay his stentorian bellow for five minutes while the guests finish their 'afters'. It will not be necessary to have soup if the main dish is hot.

The most idyllic partridge shooting that I remember in England used to be our annual invitation to shoot on the large estate which Archie looked after for many years as professional pigeon shooter. It was the quintessence of all that I used to enjoy about shooting. Our, host, hostess and their family and friends were the Guns, but thankfully there were no paying guests. We knew all the keepers and most of the beaters, and every inch of the ground as Archie had been shooting pigeons there for forty years, so each drive was like an old friend whose every move is familiar. There were not too many drives, and lunch in one of the well-appointed huts was always delicious and never rushed. If you were lucky and drew a peg near one of the plum belts you could gather ripe mirabelle plums for your favourite brew of plum brandy.

PIGEON PIE

At this time of year pigeons will be in plentiful supply and plump from the harvest, so make use of them in a pie; if the weather turns warm you can serve it cold, but it's really nicest hot. I hasten to add that this is by no means the only way to serve them. Archie and I spent many years combating what we called the 'pigeon pie mentality' by inventing more unusual ways of cooking them, but a pie can be delicious.

16 pigeon breasts (8 pigeons)
8 oz/225 g chopped onion
2 oz/50 g finely chopped carrot
2 oz/50 g finely chopped swede
4 oz/100 g pork sausage meat
10 smoked streaky bacon rashers
2 tablespoons Country Herb Stuffing (or cranberry and orange or pork and chestnut) soaked in 1 tablespoon of boiling water

1 dessertspoon cranberry or rowan jelly
¾ pint/425 ml stock or same amount of water and a stock cube
¼ pint/150 ml red wine
Seasoned flour for dredging
Salt and freshly ground black pepper
8 crushed juniper berries
1 sprig rosemary
2 bay leaves

Serves 12-16

With a sharp knife remove the pigeon breasts and cut in dice. Cook the carcasses in a pan of water with a carrot, onion, leek, celery stalk, and bouquet garni for 2 hours. Roll the pigeon dice in seasoned flour, put in a casserole with ¾ pint (425 ml) stock and ¼ pint (150 ml) red wine. Cover and place in a pre-heated oven at 300°F/150°C/Gas Mark 2 and cook for 3 hours or until it is so tender that it melts in the mouth. Allow to get completely cold and then tip it into a pie dish. Adjust seasoning if necessary. Make the sausage meat and stuffing mix into marble-sized balls and dot them over the top. Cut the rashers in half, roll them up and do the same. Lay the bay leaves and rosemary sprig across and sprinkle with juniper berries. Cover with a shortcrust pastry made with 12 oz (350 g) flour, 8 oz (225 g) butter, 2-4 tablespoons water and 1 pinch salt. Pre-heat oven to 425°F/200°C/Gas Mark 7 and put in pie. Leave for 12 minutes then turn down to 350°F/175°C/Gas Mark 4 for another 25 minutes. Remove from oven and add a little more hot stock through the centre hole. You can make the pigeon mixture and pastry ahead of time and freeze them separately, ready to cook when you need to. Serve with mashed potatoes and Lucy's Buttered Carrots.

LUCY'S BUTTERED CARROTS

One of Lucy's more extravagant dishes from her university days. I don't how she afforded it!

2 lbs/1 kg old carrots	*1 tablespoon finely chopped parsley*
2 oz/50 g butter	*Salt and freshly ground black pepper*
1 tablespoon sugar	

Peel the carrots and put them through the Alumette or fine-slicing disc of the Magimix. Put them into a saucepan with the rest of the ingredients (except the parsley), cover tightly and cook over a *very low* heat. Shake occasionally and give it the odd stir. Remove from stove when they are just cooked — still firm or *al dente* , and mix in the parsley.

VEAL or PORK CASSEROLE WITH APPLES, ONIONS, CIDER AND CALVADOS

Another of Lucy's recipes, designed when she became allergic to dairy products. The oil and sheep's yogurt actually improve it I think, but you can use butter and cream if you wish.

4 lbs/2 kg diced stewing veal or pork	*1 bottle sparkling Normandy cider*
1 lb/450 g onions, peeled and roughly chopped	*2 tablespoons Calvados (optional)*
1 lb/450 g apples, peeled and roughly chopped	*1 dessertspoon demerara sugar, apple or redcurrant jelly*
8 oz/225 g button mushrooms	*1 teaspoon green peppercorns*
Oil for sautéeing	*¼ pint/150 ml sheep's yogurt or cream*
Seasoned flour for dredging	*Salt and pepper*

Serves 12–16

Sauté the onions, apples and mushrooms in some of the oil and when just beginning to colour transfer to a casserole. Dredge the veal or pork with the flour and sauté in hot oil. Warm the Calvados, pour into the pan and light. Shake until the flames die out. Lift the meat out with a slotted spoon and add to the onions and apples. Add a little more oil to the pan and any seasoned flour left over, cook for a few minutes and then add the cider. Reduce for at least 5 minutes — it concentrates the flavour. Pour into the casserole and add the seasonings. Cover and cook in a pre-heated oven at 350°F/175°C/Gas Mark 4 for 1½ — 2 hours. Add yogurt or cream just before serving. As a change from potatoes serve with plenty of hot crusty bread and fine green beans. This dish improves if made a day or two beforehand and then re-heated; it also freezes well. It can be made with a rich stock instead of the cider but you will then lose the very special flavour.

FRENCH APPLE TART

Shortcrust Pastry	*2 tablespoons water*
8 oz/225 g flour	
5 oz/150 g butter	Filling
½ teaspoon salt	*3 lbs/1.8 kg apples peeled, cored and cut up*
1 teaspoon caster sugar	*Demerara sugar*

Serves 8-10

Make the pastry in the Magimix, roll out and leave to rest for 1 hour. Cook the apples with 1 tablespoon water and plenty of sugar until they are very thick (what the French call a 'marmelade'), beat in a little butter and leave to cool. Line a 10-inch (25-cm) flan tin with the pastry and bake in a pre-heated oven at 400°F/200°C/Gas mark 6 for 12 minutes and then at 350°F/175°C/Gas Mark 4 for a further 10 minutes. When cold fill with the apple purée and decorate with drained tinned cherries.

COLD FRENCH BREAD-AND-BUTTER PUDDING

This is a delicious French version of bread-and-butter pudding and my friend recommended that it is best made at least two days ahead of time

1 pkt biscottes or French toasts (obtainable from Sainsbury's and most supermarkets)	*6 eggs, well beaten*
Butter	*8 oz/225 g raisins soaked in rum*
2 pints/1 litre milk	*4 tablespoons caster sugar*
	1 vanilla pod

Serves 8-10

Spread butter on both sides of enough biscottes to cover a shallow oven-proof dish big enough to hold 2 pints (1 litre) and sprinkle over the rum-soaked raisins. Bring the milk, sugar and vanilla pod to the boil. Remove vanilla pod and cool slightly, then pour onto the eggs. Pour the mixture over the biscottes and raisins and place in a pre-heated oven at 400°F/200°C/Gas Mark 6 for 20 to 25 minutes. Turn down if you think it's too hot as the milk and egg mixture must not boil. It should be golden and puffed up.

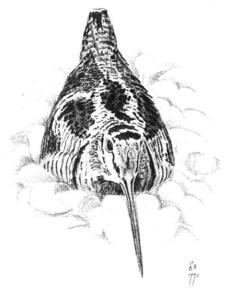

PARTRIDGE SHOOTING —
LATE AUTUMN

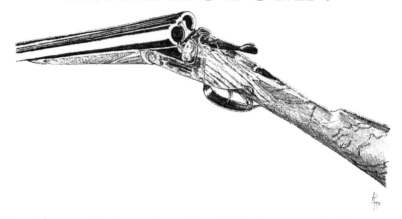

From mid-October onwards the weather will probably have turned colder, and a hot main course will be appreciated. A light casserole or stew would be a good choice, or game or poultry — but not the kind of North Country dish that sticks to your ribs, which is more suitable for keeping out the cold weather encountered on some pheasant days.

There have been occasions whilst partridge shooting in Spain when, instead of the cold collation, I have longed for a good old steak-and-kidney pudding. We stayed one year, before Tom ran the shoot commercially, in a keeper's house high up in the Sierra Moreno. It was fairly palatial and even had loos, though these were aesthetic rather than practical as there was no water and they weren't attached to anything. Your best bet was to rush out in the morning and bag the nearest bush before a beater did. As we arrived it snowed heavily and I went to bed in all my shooting gear and Archie's balaclava. That year the olive crop had failed. The beaters were so hungry that they finished up the remains of our breakfast. This explained why such hitherto punctual people had been late starting the beat. After that Tom issued them with a ration of bread, sausage and wine, something which they have never forgotten.

BREAST OF PIGEON GOODWIFE

This can equally well be made with whole pheasants prepared in this way and then cut up in to serving pieces

20 pigeon breasts (10 pigeons)	1 chicken stock cube
3 large onions cut into thick rings	1 dessertspoon cornflour mixed with a little
4 oz/100 g butter	water
6-8 tablespoons mango or Major Grey's chutney	Salt and pepper

Serves 12-16

Brown the onions in half the butter and transfer to a casserole. Seal the outsides of the pigeon breasts in the remainder of the butter and then lay them on top of the onions. Spoon the chutney over the top, season well, cover tightly and put in a pre-heated oven 300°F/150°C/Gas Mark 2 for 3 — 4 hours, or until very tender. Crumble in the stock cube and thicken the sauce with the cornflour. Personally I like to serve this dish with rice, but I have noted a decided aversion to this delectable grain among my compatriots, which I think is partly because it is so often badly cooked. Although the 'Goodwife' is not strictly a curry you could also have a bowl of spicy poppadum snacks, which are like potato crisps and come in packets. I give below my way of cooking rice. Mashed potatoes are a good alternative to mop up the sauce.

PRUE'S PERFECT RICE

This is one dish where I have the edge over Lucy. My son-in-law says she can't cook it for love or money, although I think I am gradually training her with this recipe, which shouldn't fail.

2 pkts Basmati or Pilau rice	Water
1 dessertspoon oil	Salt

Serves 12-16

Heat the oil in a large thick-bottomed saucepan until hot but not smoking, then tip in the rice and shake it well so that all the grains are coated. Pour in boiling water so that it is 2 inches above the rice. Put on the lid and place over a very low heat, if possible on a heat-reducing mat if you cook by gas. Leave for 15 — 20 minutes, turn off heat, place a folded tea-towel under the lid and leave for a further 10 minutes, then remove and fluff up the rice with a fork. It should be perfectly cooked and each grain separate.

LAMB EN DAUBE

This lamb stew from Normandy makes a change from the mass of bones floating around in flavourless liquid so often met with under the guise of Irish Stew. Although I worked for the Free French in London during the war I never actually got to France until peacetime. This recipe was given to me by French friends in Normandy on my first visit. It specified leg of lamb but cheaper cuts are equally suitable and the marinade tenderizes them anyway.

6 lbs/2½ kg leg or breast of lamb cut into	*2 carrots, cut up*
dice with all fat trimmed off	*2 shallots, sliced*
8 oz/225 g fat bacon, diced	*1 clove of garlic, peeled and slightly crushed*
4 oz/100 g butter	*2 bay leaves*
1½ pints/850 ml stock or same quantity	*1 sprig thyme*
water plus 1 lamb stock cube	*1 good sprig rosemary*
Peel from 1 orange (optional)	*¼ teaspoon nutmeg*
	1 teaspoon brown sugar
Marinade	
1 pint/575 ml red wine	*Cornflour to thicken*
½ pint/150 ml oil	*Salt and pepper*

Serves 12-16

Put the lamb into a large bowl and pour over all the marinade ingredients. Cover and put in the bottom of the fridge for 24 hours, stirring once or twice. Heat the butter in a thick casserole and brown the bacon. Strain the marinade juice from the lamb and reserve. Pat the meat dry and brown in the butter. Pour over the marinade and the stock, lay the orange peel on top, cover tightly and place in a pre-heated oven 325°F/160°C/Gas Mark 3 for 3 hours or until tender. Blot off the fat with kitchen paper and thicken with a little cornflour mixed with some cold water. Serve with plain boiled potatoes, *plenty* of garlic bread, and a watercress and orange salad to take away the richness.

MINCE WITH LASAGNE TOPPING

This makes a change from cottage pie and is less tedious to make than lasagne as you don't have to boil so many batches of pasta. If you have a glut of venison or pigeon breasts in your freezer it is a good way to use them up. It also freezes well.

4 lbs/2 kg lean minced meat of your choice	*2 oz/50 g flour*
4 oz/100 g peeled, chopped onion	*1 pint/575 ml milk*
2 tablespoons oil	*6 oz/175 g grated fresh parmesan or strong*
1 teaspoon mixed herbs	*Cheddar cheese*
1 tablespoon tomato pureé	
1 teaspoon Worcester Sauce	*Lasagne Topping*
Salt and ground black pepper	
	6—8 squares Barilla lasagne
Cheese Sauce	*4 pints/2.3 litres boiling water*
	1 tablespoon olive oil
2 oz/50 g butter	

Serves 12-16

Heat the oil in a thick frying pan and seal the mince. Transfer to a casserole, add the other ingredients and mix well. Cover and place in a pre-heated oven at 325°F/160°C/Gas Mark 3 for 3 hours or until really tender. Spoon into a large, flat, square or oblong earthenware dish — if you are really pushed you can use an aluminium roasting pan. Make a cheese sauce, but reserve at least 2 tablespoons cheese to sprinkle on top. Cook the lasagne squares in the boiling water and oil, then drain on a clean tea-towel. Cover the mince with the cheese sauce, then finally a layer of lasagne. Sprinkle with cheese and place in a pre-heated oven at 350°F/175°C/Gas Mark 4 for half an hour or until it is brown and bubbling. Serve with curly kale cooked for a short while in boiling salted water so that it is still bright green, well-drained and roughly chopped in the Magimix.

HAM IN PARSLEY SAUCE GRATINÉ

This good old English dish is most delicious. For ease of carving the smoked pork loin is the best opinion, though it is more expensive. They are obtainable from most branches of Sainsbury's and Marks and Spencer.

4-6 lbs/2-3½ kg lean collar, corner of gammon or smoked pork loin	*Parsley Sauce*
1 onion	*3 oz/75g butter*
1 carrot	*3 oz/75 g flour*
1 stalk celery	*1 pint/575 ml milk*
½ pint/275 ml white wine	*½ pint/275 ml stock from cooking liquid*
Water	*1 tablespoon chopped parsley*
1 teaspoon peppercorns	*Fresh white breadcrumbs*

Serves 12-16

Place the ham in cold water with the vegetables, wine and seasoning. Bring slowly to the boil and simmer gently for 30 minutes to the lb (450 g). Allow to get cold in the liquid then remove and cut into fairly thick slices. Lay these overlapping in a flat earthenware dish. Make a béchamel sauce, add the parsley and pour over the ham slices. Sprinkle with a layer of breadcrumbs, dot with butter and brown in a pre-heated oven at 400°F/200°C/Gas Mark 6 for about 15-20 minutes. Serve with new potatoes and tinned petits pois.

BOILED CHICKEN AND EGG SAUCE

Another good old friend which I dug out of my mother's receipt book, bringing back childhood memories as we always used to have it on a Wednesday. Menus were pretty rigid in those days and you always knew what to expect, and when. For 12-16 people you need 2 x 4 lb (1.8 kg) chickens. Follow the recipe for boiled ham above, but simmer the chickens for approximately 50 minutes then allow to cool in the liquid. When cold take out, cut up and lay on a dish. Make a béchamel sauce as in previous recipe and instead of parsley add 3 chopped hard-boiled eggs. Pour over the chicken and garnish with bacon rolls and triangles of fried bread. These can be cooked and then heated up in the oven at the last minute. Serve with sauté potatoes and string beans.

PHEASANT SHOOTING — LUNCH AT HOME

OCTOBER AND NOVEMBER

Lunch at home is, compared to some other venues, a piece of cake, so to speak. No worrying whether you've brought enough soup, forgotten the whisky, or whether if you sneak a sandwich out of each lunch box there'll be enough for that extra girlfriend who turned up unexpectedly. All you have to do is to plan the menu, cook it, keep it hot, organize the drinks and lay the table. Everything is nice and conventional and you don't need to improvize. Early in the season the afternoons are not so short and you can probably afford the time to provide a pudding, but cheese and biscuits should be on the table for those who do not have a sweet tooth. It really is best to dish out the food yourself as by the time everyone has milled around with before-lunch drinks and finally been shepherded into the dining room a lot of precious eating time has been lost; a lot more will also have been wasted by well-mannered gentlemen saying 'after you'.

There are two kinds of lunch at home, the sit-down, and the buffet or what I have called 'The Four O' Clock Feast', for which I have given an 'ops' plan later on in the book (see pp. 73-5). If you, the cook, are also a vital 'stopping' or beating cog in the shoot you will have to do a lot of what Archie always referred to as 'forward thinking'. If this is the case plan your menu so that the main course will take care of itself in the oven or on the hot-plate.

THE NIGHT BEFORE: Lay the table, put out the drinks, peel the vegetables and put in salted water in bottom of fridge. Wash and drain salads, put in bowls and cover with cling-film. Make dressing(s). Make any last-minute dishes such as mousses or puddings which can't be made ahead of time and frozen. Get any pâtés/terrines or other items out of the freezer.

CRACK OF DAWN ON THE DAY: Put butter on table covered with cling-film (it's horrid when rock hard). Take French bread or rolls out of freezer. Put ice in bucket, and put out a lemon with a knife to cut it. Check there is beer for the beaters. Large bowl of water outside for dogs. Hose and brush handy for dirty boots when guests leave.

JUST BEFORE 'THE OFF': Put casserole in oven and switch on LOW or AUTO. It's easy to forget as I did once for one of the Tower Hill shoots — it was quite a problem to know how I was going to heat up a gallon of cassoulet in 30 minutes!

HALF AN HOUR BEFORE LUNCH: Take casserole out of oven and put on hot-plate. Cook vegetables. Put bread in oven to heat up. Take pâté/terrine/mousse, or starter if you are having one, out of fridge, also cheese(s). The flavours are not released until they are at room temperature. Put beer, opened wine, on table. Drain vegetables, add butter or whatever. Take everything into the dining room, have a strong drink, heave a sigh of relief and call in the guests.

SALMI OF OXTAIL AND WILD DUCK

This may seem rather a strange marriage of ingredients, but it is quite a useful way of using up some of last year's duck which may be lurking in your deep-freeze. More important, it is very delicious.

2 oxtails jointed and trimmed of all fat	*2-3 bay leaves*
2 mallard	*1 sprig each thyme and rosemary*
1 large onion, unpeeled and stuck with	*1 tablespoon redcurrant jelly*
cloves	*2 tablespoons tomato purée*
1 onion, cut up	*8 oz/225 g oyster mushrooms*
2 carrots, sliced in rounds	*1 bottle hearty red wine*
2 leeks, sliced in rounds	*Oil for sautéeing*
3 cloves of garlic	*Flour for dredging*
1 teaspoon mixed herbs	*Salt and pepper*

Serves 12–16

Put the oxtails in a large pan with carrot, onion, celery and leek and cover with cold water. Bring to the boil slowly and simmer for 15 minutes, skimming constantly. Leave the very small bony joints in the stock and take out the others. Drain well and dry. Coat in flour and brown together with the onion, carrots and leeks in the oil. Put in a casserole, pour in the wine and top up with stock to cover and add the herbs, jelly and seasoning. Place in a pre-heated oven at 275°F/140°C/Gas Mark 1 for 5-6 hours. Joint the ducks, dredge with flour and brown in oil. Add them to the oxtail 3 hours before the end of cooking. Blot all the fat off with squares of kitchen paper and if you don't think it is thick enough add some cornflour mixed with a little water. Best made the day before. Freezes well. As it is very rich you only need mashed potato or crusty French bread to accompany it and a frisée salad. If there is any left over you can pour in the stock, swill it round and simmer for 2 hours. Then scrape off any meat, discard the bones and when cold put it away in the freezer as a basis for Oxtail Soup (see p.65).

TRICK OF THE TRADE. To remove fat from any stock, soup or casserole. Draw squares of kitchen paper across the surface. The fat or grease will adhere and you can throw it away. You may need to use nearly a roll for a large oxtail stew.

TRICK OF THE TRADE. Instead of cornflour you can add a packet of oxtail soup, it makes for added richness; you can also cheat and use it in other beef stews if they need a bit more 'oomph'.

VENISON STEW

This takes care of all the other bits of a beast except the haunches, which are best roasted. It makes a change from beef or lamb and can easily be cooked ahead of time and frozen for future use.

4-6 lbs/1.8-3½ kg diced venison	1 teaspoon dried thyme
1 lb/450 g fat salt pork cut into dice	1 teaspoon juniper berries
1 pig's trotter	1 pint/575 ml venison stock (see below)
1 lb/450 g onion, peeled and chopped	½ pint/275 ml Guinness
1 lb/450 g carrots cut into rounds	Oil for frying
1 dessertspoon dark muscovado sugar	Salt and pepper

Serves 12-16

Brown the onions and carrots in some oil then transfer to a casserole. Sauté the diced salt pork and finally the venison. Add to the vegetables, season and pour in the stock and Guinness, lay the pig's trotter on top, cover and cook in a pre-heated oven at 300°F/150°C/Gas Mark 2 for 2 hours or until tender. Blot the fat off with kitchen paper, remove the trotter and thicken with Beurre Manié (see below). Serve with glazed kohlrabi or turnips and new potatoes.

BEURRE MANIÉ

Knead together equal quantities of butter and flour or, better still, whizz them in the Magimix. Drop tiny pieces into stew or soup and stir or whisk until it is thick enough.

VENISON STOCK

Roast all the venison bones with some chopped carrot and onion in a little oil in a very hot oven until they are a nice dark brown colour, then place in a saucepan, cover with water, drop in a bouquet garni, season and cook for 4-5 hours on a very low heat. Strain and use or freeze.

BEEF ROLY-POLY

This recipe came from the redoubtable Sophy, who used to reign over Archie's cousin's kitchen. In the early days when we stayed there, I remember that the butler used to take the shoot lunch down to the house of one of the tenant farmers. It was a full-scale affair with silver, china, glass and napery, and he waited on us. As I rush back from beating to organise our lunch, I often think of those days with envy.

Pastry	Filling
1 lb/450 g self-raising flour	*1 lb/450 g lean raw minced beef*
1 teaspoon salt	*4 oz/100 g finely chopped onion*
8 oz/225 g shredded suet	*1 level teaspoon mixed herbs*
10-12 tablespoons water	*1 dessertspoon chopped parsley*
	4-6 tablespoons good stock or gravy

Serves 8-10

Mix pastry, divide in half and roll each piece out to a rectangle roughly 10 x 12 inches (25 x 30 cm). Mix the mince with the herbs, seasoning and gravy and spread over each rectangle to within 1 inch (3 cm) of the edge. Moisten all round with water and roll up from the shorter sides. Wrap in foil and steam for 2 hours. Serve with boiled onions, carrots and potatoes.

RAY'S MINCE AND HERBY DUMPLINGS

A friend who was in the same shooting party in Spain last season gave me this delicous and filling recipe. At the time, sitting over our alfresco and vinous feast, relaxing in the sun, it was hard to contemplate the need for such a 'strengthening' main course, but once back in England the idea became very attractive.

4 lbs/2 kg lean mince	3 oz/75 g shredded suet
8 oz/225 g chopped onion	2 level teaspoons baking powder
2 tablespoons oil	1 level teaspoon salt
1 teaspoon mixed herbs	1 dessertspoon chopped parsley
1 teaspoon redcurrant jelly	1 teaspoon mixed herbs
1 teaspoon Worcester Sauce	1 egg, beaten
Salt and black pepper	1 teaspoon lemon juice
	Ground black pepper
Herby Dumplings	Water
8 oz/225 g plain flour	

Serves 10-12

To cook the mince follow the method for Mince with Lasagne Topping (p.41). Just before you are due to take the mince out of the oven make the dumplings.

For the Herby Dumplings, sieve together the flour, baking powder and salt in a bowl. Sprinkle in the parsley, herbs and suet and grind on some black pepper. Make a well in the centre and mix in the egg, lemon juice and enough water to make a soft dough. Remove the mince from the oven and turn the heat up to 450°F/230°C/Gas Mark 8. Spoon the meat into a large shallow earthenware dish. Make dessertspoonfuls of suet pastry into balls, roll in flour and arrange on the mince. Cover with foil and place in the oven for 10 minutes — the dumplings will cook in the steam and swell. Take the foil off for the last 10 minutes for them to get brown and crisp. Curly kale, cooked for 4 minutes in boiling salted water without a lid, drained and then whizzed in the Magimix for a few seconds goes well, and, if you must, have potatoes just plainly boiled.

CASSOULET

This is a wonderful dish as you can adapt it to the ingredients that are available. I had it first in the Tarn with an ex-Free French friend who had an estate there. It is the heart of the Armagnac country. When Charles returned after the war his first thought was of his Armagnac, so he went to see his old cellarman, Joseph, and asked how the twenty-year old blend was getting on. 'Ah! Monsieur, taste it, it is as if the Good God was walking down your throat in velvet trousers.' Don't be put off, it's not as complicated as it looks and however conservative your guests may be, once they've tasted it they'll ask for more. It is a real peasant dish and as such is perfect for a lot of hungry people on a cold day.

3 lbs/1.4 kg haricot beans	1 tube tomato purée
12 oz/350 g garlic sausage	3 fat cloves garlic, finely chopped
1½ lbs/675 g bacon or salt pork cut into cubes	1 lb/450 g small onions (the pickling variety)
1 pig's trotter	3 pints/1½ litres bean water
2 lbs/900 g lamb breast cut into cubes	½ pint/275 ml red wine
4 duck breasts cut in slices lengthways, or Confit d'Oie (see below)	Basil, rosemary, thyme, bay leaves
2 lbs/900 g pork loin cut into cubes	Fresh breadcrumbs
12 oz/350 g smoked sausage	Salt and ground black pepper

Serves 12–16

Don't faint at the number of ingredients, you can add or subtract or substitute. Duck breasts or Magret of duck are usually obtainable at supermarkets, but if you think they're too pricey use a couple of wild duck, partially roasted and cut into serving pieces, or, if you have been lumbered with a wild goose which is lurking unloved and unwanted in the freezer, why not try making it into Confit d'Oie (see below), for it is one of the classic ingredients of this wonderful dish from the Languedoc.

TEAL

Soak the beans overnight, then tip into a saucepan with their water, 2 onions, 2 cloves garlic, sprig of thyme, 2 bay leaves, salt and pepper, and cook gently for 1 hour, or until nearly tender. Poach the garlic sausage for 15 minutes in bean water then take out and slice. Brown the meats, smoked sausage and onions, separately. Cut up the sausage into slices. In the bottom of a large earthenware casserole spread a layer of lamb and pork loin, then a layer of haricot beans, the browned onions, more haricot beans, then the strips of duck breast or pieces of goose and bacon, more beans, then the smoked and garlic sausage, ending up with a thin layer of beans. Swill the sauté pan out with the red wine, add the chopped garlic, tomato purée, herbs, salt and pepper and enough bean water to make up to 2 pints (1 litre). Pour carefully into the casserole. Put a 2-inch (5-cm) layer of breadcrumbs over the top and place in a pre-heated oven at 300°F/150°C/Gas Mark 2 for 4-6 hours. If it dries out during cooking, carefully pour some more bean water down the side of the casserole. The longer and slower it is cooked the better. A mixed green salad is the only accompaniment needed.

CONFIT D'OIE SAUVAGE

As a wild goose will not render enough fat it will have to be cooked in pork dripping or lard. Cut the goose into pieces and rub all over with coarse sea salt. Put into a dish and leave in the bottom of the fridge for 5-6 days. Rinse well, dry and lay in a thick saucepan. Melt the pork dripping or lard and pour over the bird, put on the lid and simmer very gently for 3-4 hours until *completely tender*. Take out the pieces of goose and lay in oblong foil dishes, then pour the cooking fat over them. When quite cold, cover and freeze. The classic way was to put the pieces in a large earthenware crock, cover them with fat, tie paper over the top and keep them in a cool larder or cellar. When you wanted one or two pieces to jazz up a dish, you just took them out and poured over some more melted fat. In this way they kept for up to three months. Nowadays, with the fear of salmonella, it seems safer to freeze them; anyway most of us have no larders, worse luck!

TOAD IN THE HOLE

A sadly rare dish nowadays which needs reviving. Only to be attempted in your house or somewhere with an oven. For some reason it is not successful in a fan-assisted oven. Try and find really well-flavoured spicy sausages — not the bland, uniform ones generally available — if you can manage it. See if you can suss out a speciality sausage made by a local butcher. Serve with Bubble and Squeak (see below).

3 lbs/1.4 kg Lincolnshire or plain pork sausages	2 pints/1 litre skimmed milk
12 oz/350 g plain flour	1 level teaspoon salt
4 eggs	Lard or dripping

Serves 8-10

Sieve the flour and salt into a large bowl, make a well in the centre and break in the eggs. Beat them in and add enough milk to make a batter like thick cream. Beat well with electric beaters, if you have them. Cover and leave to stand for 1 hour. Brown the sausages in a frying pan. Set the oven to 425°F/220°C/Gas Mark 7. Pour 3-4 tablespoons fat from the sausages into a large roasting pan and heat in the oven. Beat the batter once more and pour it into the pan and put in the sausages. As soon as the batter has risen and puffed up turn the heat down to 375°F/190°C/Gas Mark 5. Cook for 40 minutes altogether. Serve in the roasting tin.

BUBBLE AND SQUEAK

This was of course a frugal way of using up leftovers. Lucy's old nanny used to be horrified that none of her neighbours ate the Sunday roast cold, and would never have considered making cottage pie or the like. She brought up six children on £2 a week and had herself gone out to work aged twelve for one shilling a week, so she knew what she was talking about.

1 cabbage, preferably Savoy	Salt and pepper
3 lbs/1.4 kg peeled potatoes	Fat for frying

Serves 8-10

Cut the potatoes into quarters and boil in salted water until cooked. Mash roughly. Cut the cabbage up coarsely and cook in boiling salted water until tender. Drain well. To get the authentic taste you should really do this the day before and leave the vegetables to get cold. Heat some fat or dripping in your largest frying pan, or even two. When really hot put in a mixture of potato and cabbage. When brown and crisp on the bottom, turn it over with a spatula. You won't get it over in one piece. No matter, just continue until most of what was on the bottom is now on top. You may have to add some more fat. Loosen the bottom with a spatula and turn onto a heated dish.

APPLE CHARLOTTE

My son-in-law is not nicknamed 'Piggy' for nothing, and when we stay with Auntie Constance, Lucy's godmother, she always produces a succession of what are known as 'Piggy puddings'. This is one of them, and I have known him to have three helpings or more.

---

4 lbs/1.8 kg apples   *Softened butter*
Stale white bread   *Demerara sugar*

Serves 8–10

Pre-heat oven to 350°F/175°C/Gas Mark 4. Peel, core and cut apples into thick slices. Butter bread slices on both sides and line a large pie-dish with them. Fill with apples, sugar and buttered bread slices in layers, ending up with the bread on top. Sprinkle thickly with sugar and a dusting of cinnamon powder. Bake for 40–50 minutes and serve with double cream.

ANN'S WINTER SUMMER PUDDING

A friend of mine in the village went berserk one year at a pick-your-own-fruit place. There was such a surplus that she made it into Kissel (see below). This is a kind of thickened fruit compôte from Austria. The following year she came upon all this Kissel in the freezer and wondered what to do with it. Her answer was to make a hot Summer Pudding. It's very simple, just follow the recipe above, but instead of raw apple use layers of Kissel.

KISSEL

4 lbs/1.8 kg mixture of blackcurrants, redcurrants, stoned cherries, raspberries, strawberries	8 oz/225 g sugar (or more to taste) 2 tablespoons arrowroot

Serves 8-10

Cook the fruit with a little water. Add the sugar and dissolve. Mix the arrowroot with a little water and add to the fruit, bring back to the boil and stir constantly. Cool and use as a fruit compôte or in Ann's Winter Summer Pudding. Freezes well.

RICH CREAMY RICE PUDDING

You might like to make this to go with the Kissel. Try the French tip of cooking it with a bay leaf instead of cinnamon or nutmeg.

2 pints/1 litre milk 4 oz/100 g round-grained pudding rice 8 oz/225 g sugar	1 bay leaf 1 oz/25 g butter

Serves 6-8

Butter a shallow earthernware dish with a 4-pint/2-litre capacity. Sprinkle in the rice. Heat up the milk with the bay leaf, sugar and a pinch of salt. Stir well and when it begins to boil pour over the rice. Cover the top with little bits of butter. Place in the middle of a pre-heated oven at 275°F/140°C/Gas Mark 2. Stir the pudding every half an hour. (You can only make this pudding if you are not actively involved in the shoot.) When the rice is tender and creamy move the dish to the top shelf and bake until it is a rich golden brown. Serve with a big bowl of Kissel and gild the lily with some cream.

JAM OR TREACLE LAYER PUDDING

I notice that men love all these old-fashioned puddings. However much we are preached at to eat healthily I think it's lovely to break out once in a while. After a cold morning with a biting wind, or driving rain which has managed to penetrate the defences of your Barbour, there will never be a better excuse to tuck into a helping of light, meltingly delicious steamed suet pudding.

Suet Pastry	Pinch salt
8 oz/225 g flour	3 oz/75 g shredded suet
1 teaspoon baking powder	Cold water to mix

Serves 6-8

Sift together the flour, salt and baking powder, sprinkle in suet and mix to a soft dough with the water. Roll out just over half the pastry into a round. Butter a pudding basin and sprinkle with demerara sugar and line with the pastry. Put a layer of jam or treacle at the bottom and then a layer of suet crust. Fill up alternately, ending with suet crust. Dampen the edge to seal firmly. Cover with greaseproof paper or foil and steam for 2 hours or longer. For a shooting party of 12-16 you may have to make another one of this size, or 1 large one — just double the quantities. If using treacle sprinkle a few breadcrumbs on each layer and a squeeze of lemon juice or a pinch of ginger.

PHEASANT SHOOTING —
LUNCH IN A SHOOTING HUT

Shooting huts come in all shapes and sizes, from a purpose-built job with all mod. cons., to a deserted keeper's house, to a draughty barn with straw bales. The following recipes are designed for the kind of hut that has chairs and trestle tables, but no cooking facilities. The 'all mod. con.' ones rate the same kind of menu, or adaptation thereof, to the sort of thing you would produce in your own house. For all kinds of shooting hut you will have to remember to take cutlery, glasses, a cold-box and ice for the pre-lunch drinks, plates and soup bowls, and tablecloths. Wide-mouthed thermoses are a must as the only hot food you will be able to produce will be an all-in-one stew or main-course soup with plenty of nourishing bits in it.

After leaving school Lucy went out to help with the catering at her godfather's commercial shooting enterprise in Spain. In wet weather late on in the season the wonderful alfresco affairs became a wistful memory. Lucy and the two waiters, Baldomero and Felipe, used to home in on one of the local farmers and bribe him to provide a room with an open hearth. Somehow or other the trestle tables would be fitted in to accommodate anything up to twenty-six people, wood and dried herb bushes would be gathered, the fire lit and tables set. Preparation of the hors d'oeuvres might take place on an open windowsill (workspace being limited) and, when the fire was hot enough, the four-legged iron grid would be placed over it and the chops or stew cooked on it. Smoke usually billowed out as the chimney might not have been used for years, but when the wet hunters came in a plentiful slurping of 103 brandy usually made all troubles vanish. One peculiarity was the sweetened, condensed milk which came round, still in its tin, with the coffee. Guns or wives could often be seen surreptitiously dipping in their spoons (or fingers), and when caught out they looked sheepish and said it either made them remember their school days or the war, depending on how old they were.

CHECK LIST
2 - 3 x 1 litre wide-mouthed thermoses
1 large cold-box for drinks
1 - 2 insulated bags
Plenty of newspaper and, if possible, bubble wrap
1 polystyrene fish box if possible for hot French bread/rolls
Appropriate number of tumblers, glass or plastic
Glasses for 'winter warmers' or port
Soup bowls
Plates, cutlery
Salt, pepper, sugar
Cheese dish, take biscuits in tin
Covered butter dish(es)
Basket or similar for French bread/rolls
Basket or dish for fruit
Tablecloth(s) (optional)
Paper napkins
Plastic container of water for dogs, plus bowls — if it's very cold the water may be frozen and there may not be a tap.

SCANDINAVIAN YELLOW SPLIT PEA SOUP WITH PORK

This recipe was given to me by Archie's half-Swedish niece. It is traditionally eaten in every Swedish home at least once a week. A good stock makes it that much more delicious, and ham stock is best. If you haven't got any make do with ham stock cubes.

1½ lbs/675 g dried yellow split peas	½ celeriac peeled and cut into dice
4 pints/2 litres stock	3 carrots diced
3 lbs/1.4 kg slightly salted breast or side of pork	½ teaspoon mixed herbs
	½ teaspoon dried thyme
2 onions coarsely chopped	1 level teaspoon ground ginger
2 leeks cut in rings	1 teaspoon sugar
8 oz/225 g potatoes cut in small dice	Salt and pepper

Serves 12–16

Soak the peas overnight then strain and simmer in 4 pints (2 litres) water. When tender, about 2 hours, drain and process in the Magimix. While the peas are cooking, put the pork into a saucepan, cover with cold water and bring to the boil. Skim well and simmer gently for 1½ hours. Add all the vegetables, herbs and seasoning and continue cooking until tender. Remove meat and cut into cubes. Add stock and puréed peas to pork liquid, vegetables and the diced pork meat. You can also add boiled Cumberland, smoked or garlic sausage cut in pieces to give more body. Serve with cooked beetroot, pumpernickel or rye bread, and lager or beer.

MAIN-COURSE MINESTRONE

This soup can be varied according to what is in season and you can use your imagination. The only stipulation is that it must be really thick and full of assorted vegetables and pasta.

2 onions, roughly chopped
2 carrots, diced
2 stalks celery, diced
2 potatoes, peeled and diced
1 fennel bulb, finely chopped
2 tomatoes, peeled, de-seeded and chopped
2 tablespoons peas or chopped fine French
beans or even runner beans
2 cloves garlic, peeled and finely chopped

½ teaspoon each oregano and basil (fresh
if possible)
Oil
4 pints/2 litres water or stock
4 tablespoons tomato purée
3-4 handfuls scrunched-up spaghetti or
tagliatelli
4 tablespoons grated fresh Parmesan cheese
4 tablespoons pesto sauce

Sauté the vegetables in a large thick pan in some oil, add the water or stock and cook until tender. Add the pasta, which must be broken into spoon-sized pieces or you'll have your guests struggling with streamers of spaghetti down their best shooting suits (mud or blood is acceptable, but not foreign fripperies). Cook until tender, then add the pesto sauce, which is usually obtainable in jars at the big supermarkets, and the cheese, but don't let it boil or the pesto sauce will separate. Provide more cheese for people to add if they wish. Serve with French bread which you can heat in foil in the oven, wrap in newspaper and then bubble wrap, and bring in an insulated bag. If the soup doesn't look solid enough add some chopped cooked chicken, ham or mince.

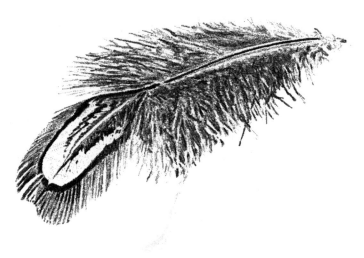

GARBURE

This is a delicious thick soup from the Basque region. This recipe was given to me by my Free French friend Charles, who said it had often kept him alive when being hunted by the Gestapo. It was a staple food of the peasants who, even during the Occupation, managed to get most of the ingredients, if not always the pork.

1 lb/450 g potatoes, peeled and cut up
1 lb/450 g haricot beans
1 lb/450 g onions, coarsely chopped
2 turnips or swedes, peeled and cut up
8 oz/225 g broad beans
8 oz/225 g peas

8 oz/225 g tomatoes, peeled, de-seeded and chopped
1 small cabbage, blanched and sliced
2 lb/1 kg belly of pork
6 pints/3 litres water
Salt and pepper

Serves 12-16

Brown the onions in some pork dripping, or goose fat if you have attempted the Confit d'Oie on p.50. Add all the other vegetables and the belly of pork. Pour on 6 pints (3 litres) water, season well and cook over a low heat until the pork is tender. Take it out and cut up into cubes. Return to the soup. Add any kind of sausage which takes your fancy, some cubes of ham and some Confit d'Oie, or cold roast wild duck or goose if you have any. Technically it should be served in a huge pot with alternate layers of slices of bread, cheese and vegetables, with the final layer being cheese and browned in the oven. As this will not be possible in your cooker-less hovel you will have to provide rounds of French bread and grated Cheddar cheese to float on top. The original recipe specified onions, potatoes and cabbage, and left the rest to the imagination and what fresh vegetables were available.

GOULASH SOUP

This a less expensive version of goulash as you can use stewing veal instead of leg of veal. Give this to your shooting guests who also ski and they will have nostaligic memories of piping hot *Gulashsuppe*, as served on a snowy mountain top.

4 lbs/1.8 kg stewing veal cut up small
2 lbs/900 g potatoes, peeled and cut up
2 lbs/900 g tomatoes, peeled, de-seeded and
cut up
2 sweet red and green peppers finely
chopped (optional)
2 cloves garlic, crushed

2 oz/50g flour
1 teaspoon ground allspice
1 teaspoon ground coriander
1 teaspoon mixed herbs
1½ oz/40 g paprika
4 pints/2 litres stock or water and stock cube
Salt and pepper

Serves 12-16

Brown the onions in a casserole then fry the veal which you have rolled in the flour, garlic and seasonings — sprinkle any left over into the casserole. Add the rest of the vegetables and the stock. Cook over a very low heat for 3 hours or until tender. Add some sour cream, yogurt or fromage frais and a dessertspoonful of caraway seeds. Serve with rye bread or pumpernickel.

GOLDEN PLOVER

ROMANY SOUP

This is a godsend for anyone who, halfway through the season, suddenly finds that there is no space in the freezer for the next batch of game. Dig down and unearth as varied a selection as you can — the more the merrier, and soon you'll have the kind of broth we all fancifully imagine bubbling away in the big black pot hanging on its tripod over a fire outside a gaily painted Romany caravan, or perhaps the kind of stew of which Toad ate so many helpings when he escaped from prison dressed as a poor washerwoman.

1 pheasant (perhaps a 'dodgy' or badly shot one)	*6 rashers smoked streaky bacon*
2 pigeons	*2 tablespoons flour*
2 legs of rabbit	*1 dessertspoon tomato purée*
1 thigh of hare	*2 sprigs fresh or 1 teaspoon dried thyme*
1 piece of stewing venison	*6 crushed juniper berries*
1 onion unpeeled and stuck with cloves	*1 tablespoon rowan jelly*
2 turnips, peeled and cut up or 1 medium swede	*1 bottle cheap red wine*
Lard or bacon fat	*3 pints/1½ litres water*
	Salt and pepper

Serves 12–16

Melt the fat in a roasting pan in a hot oven 400°F/200°C/Gas Mark 6 and then put in all the birds and bits of game that you have been able to muster. Shake well and roast until well browned, about 15 minutes. Take out and put in a large stewpan or saucepan. Sprinkle flour into the roasting pan and bubble on top of the stove for a few seconds. Pour in the wine and scrape well. Add vegetables browned in a little fat and all the other ingredients to the game. Cover and cook long and slowly, for a minimum of 2 hours. Fish out all the birds and beasts, remove the flesh and cut up, take out any bones which may have become submerged in the soup and then put back the meat. Adjust the seasoning; add cornflour slaked in a little water if it's not thick enough.

To go with these soups you should have plenty of French bread or rolls, heated in foil before you leave home, and some garlic bread if you like. Baked potatoes are another possibility, and if foil-wrapped before baking will retain their heat in an insulated bag. All else you need are a really good piece of Stilton, some proper Cheddar, with celery on the table, and Tania's Boil and Bake Fruit Cake, apples and chocolate.

TANIA'S BOIL AND BAKE FRUIT CAKE

Not being overfond of cakes or cake-making myself I can assure you that this recipe is
really easy.

1 cup of sugar	1 teaspoon mixed spice
2 cups of raisins, sultanas and currants	1 cup plain flour
mixed	1 cup self-raising flour
2 oz/50 g butter	1 teaspoon bicarbonate of soda
1 cup cold water	½ cup boiling water
½ teaspoon salt	

Serves 8–10

Put sugar, fruit, butter, cold water, spice and salt in a pan and boil for 3 minutes. Sift in
flour and mix well. Dissolve bicarbonate of soda in the boiling water and stir into cake
mixture. Put into a buttered 8-inch (20-cm) tin and cook in a pre-heated oven at
350°F/175°C/Gas Mark 4 for 1 hour.

DATE LOAF

8 oz/225 g chopped dates	1 cup boiling water
2 tablespoons butter	1 well-beaten egg
¾ cup sugar	1¾ cups self-raising flour
1 teaspoon bicarbonate of soda	

Serves 8–10

Cook dates, butter, sugar and soda in boiling water for 2 - 3 minutes. Add eggs and flour.
Cool. Grease an oblong loaf tin, spoon in ingredients, and bake for ¾ hour in a pre-heated
oven at 350°F/175°C/Gas Mark 4.

LINDA'S SPICED APPLE CAKE

On Archie's Woodmarsh shoot there is nowhere to have lunch except some rather rat-ridden barns. A friend takes pity on us and we all squash into his kitchen, which has a fabulous wood-burning stove. There's not much room for manoeuvre so 'finger food' is an essential. Linda, one of our ace beaters/pickers-up, always produces this lovely cake.

1 lb/450 g cooking apples, peeled, cored and chopped	*12 oz/350 g self-raising flour*
8 oz/225 g sultanas	*2 teaspoons cinnamon*
¼ pint/150 ml milk	*6 oz/175 g butter or margarine*
6 oz/175 g soft brown sugar	*1 egg, well beaten*
	1 oz/25 g demerara sugar

Serves 8-10

Mix together apples, sultanas, milk and sugar. Sieve together flour and cinnamon. Melt butter and mix with flour and cinnamon then add the fruit mixture and finally the egg. Stir well to combine everything thoroughly. Spoon into a buttered square cake tin lined with greaseproof paper. Sprinkle with demerara sugar and bake in a pre-heated oven at 325°F/170°C/Gas Mark 3 for 1½ hours, until risen and golden brown. It can also be served hot with cream.

PHEASANT SHOOTING — LUNCH FROM A LAND-ROVER

Let us assume that there is no lunch hut, draughty barn, or shelter of any kind. You have to produce lunch for eight Guns and their appendages. They will have to sit on their shooting-sticks, stand, or, if they are lucky enough, shelter in their own vehicles. But if it is the sort of shoot of which I am thinking they will have been ferried about in some kind of converted truck, and so will have nowhere to hide from the elements. Anyway they will feel it anti-social not to be with their fellow guests. With these criteria to work from you will have to provide a concentrated and nutritious soup thin enough to be drunk from a cup, and plenty of appetising — and, if possible, hot — goodies to eat. Pre-lunch drinks are a must and should be offered as soon as you screech up in your Land-Rover. Get these dished out as soon as possible because lunch will not take as long as it normally does and the host/shoot captain will have no trouble in rallying his troops for the afternoon drives — they will be only too thankful to get moving again. Bring two or three shallow cardboard boxes — tomato boxes are ideal. Line with tea-towels and fill with an assortment of sandwiches/buns/hot snacks. Cover the lot with a clean blanket. One of the boxes should contain apples, chocolate and a good rib-sticking fruit cake. This is an occasion when coffee is probably called for, so when you judge that people have had enough to eat, hand some round. It is certainly a good idea to have someone to help you dish things out, as speed is of the essence and once all your guests have had something to eat and drink they will be less likely to notice the inhospitable surroundings. This is also definitely the time for that special brew of sloe gin that you made. As soon as you produce it many of the male guests will suddenly whip out flasks containing 'own recipe' knock-outs. It never ceases to amaze me that the most unlikely men go to the trouble of brewing their own particular potions, and swear blind that it was all their 'own unaided work'.

CHECK LIST
2-3 (2-pint) 1.8-litre thermoses
Insulated bag containing boxes of hot snacks
Cardboard tomato trays lined with clean tea-towels
Blanket or old quilted sleeping-bag to put over top of trays
Tumblers (glass or plastic)
Plastic soup mugs
Whisky, gin, tonic, water, beer
Sloe gin or similar
Fruit cake, chocolate, apples

OXTAIL SOUP

If you haven't got any left-over oxtail/duck stock in the deep freeze you'll have to start from scratch, but you can do a wonderful quick cheat with packet soup — and that goes for quite a lot of other kinds of soup, even the ubiquitous tomato.

1 oxtail	*2 tablespoons tomato purée*
1 unpeeled onion stuck with cloves	*1 tablespoon redcurrant jelly*
1 carrot, chopped	*1 teaspoon mixed herbs*
1 leek, cut up	*1 beef stock cube (optional)*
1 stalk celery	*A good slosh of sherry (optional)*
½ swede, peeled and roughly cut up	*Flour for dredging*
2 unpeeled cloves garlic	*Oil for frying*
3 pints/1½ litres water	*Salt and ground black pepper*
1 bottle cheap red wine	

Serves 10-12

Trim the fat off the oxtail, roll in flour and brown in some oil. Put into a large saucepan or casserole together with all the other ingredients except the sherry. Simmer very gently either on top of the stove or in the oven for 4–5 hours — the longer the better. If you have a solid fuel cooker leave in the slow oven overnight. Strain and de-grease with squares of kitchen paper, add the stock cube at this point if it seems to need a boost. Re-heat and if it is a very cold day reinforce with a slosh of sherry.

TRICK OF THE TRADE. The 'quick cheat' I mentioned:

2 packets oxtail soup	½ teaspoon ground bay leaves
1 small tin tomato soup	2 cloves garlic pushed through a garlic
4 pints/2.3 litres water or good stock	press, or well crushed
½ pint/275 ml port or sweet sherry	1 tablespoon redcurrant jelly
½ teaspoon mixed herbs	Salt and pepper

Heat stock or water. Mix contents of packets with port or sherry and add together with all the other ingredients. Simmer for 15 minutes.

CURRIED CHICKEN SOUP

This is a kind of Mulligatawny soup, well spiced but not too hot as, unlike the Coats family, most people's taste buds are not so attuned to very hot food.

8 oz/225 g very finely ground cooked chicken	1 dessertspoon brown sugar
2 large onions, very finely chopped	1 dessertspoon cream of coconut
2 large cooking apples, peeled and finely chopped	1 tablespoon sultanas
	1 teaspoon mixed herbs
4 peeled cloves garlic, finely chopped	1 teaspoon curry powder
4 pints/2.3 litres chicken stock	1 teaspoon turmeric
1 cup rice (any kind)	½ teaspoon ground cumin
1 tablespoon mango chutney	Salt and pepper
	Oil for frying

Serves 10–12

Fry the chopped onion and apple in the oil until brown. Add the spices and cook for a few seconds, stirring constantly. Add some of the stock and let it bubble for a few minutes, scraping and stirring. Transfer to a large saucepan and add all the other ingredients. Simmer until tender, about half an hour. Liquidize until smooth and adjust the seasoning. If too sweet add a squeeze of lemon juice. Do try to use a really good, well-flavoured stock. The rice should thicken it enough, but if not add a little cornflour mixed with some water.

SHOOTING-STICK FOOD

SAUSAGE PARCEL

1 lb/450 g pork sausagemeat	½ teaspoon Worcester Sauce or mushroom
2 oz/50 g porridge oats	ketchup
2 tablespoons, apple, tomato or fruit	3 hard-boiled eggs
chutney	Salt and pepper
½ teaspoon dry mustard	

Serves 6

Mix all the ingredients together and add any more seasoning that your imagination dictates — finely chopped apple, walnut, a pinch of ground cumin, or what you will. On a floured board press the mixture into a rectangle, place the eggs down the centre and fold the sides over the top making a giant sausage. Oil some foil, place the roll on it and wrap. Place in a pre-heated oven at 375°F/190°C/Gas Mark 5 and cook for 30 minutes. Pull back the foil and allow it to brown for 15 minutes. Cool and cut into slices, or use as a filling for a bap with plenty of Dijon mustard.

SAUTÉED CHICKEN LIVERS IN CRISPY BAPS

Sauté some chicken livers and bacon in butter. Chop the chicken livers and bacon and spoon into baps (see p.14). Top with a few slices of tomato and onion. Season and put on the 'hats'.

GLADYS'S SCOTCH EGGS

Gladys is my tower of strength, and without her I should never have managed when Archie became crippled. When her brother retired she had a party — and these are some of the delicious goodies she made.

8-10 small hard-boiled eggs	*Beaten egg*
2 lbs/900 g peeled potatoes	*Breadcrumbs*
Butter	*Oil for frying*
Flour	

Boil the potatoes, drain and mash well, add butter, salt and pepper and mix until you have a malleable mass. Scoop out a tablespoon or so at a time, roll into a ball with floured hands, press an egg into it, mould the potato mixture around it, coat with egg and breadcrumbs and fry in deep fat until golden. Serve whole or cut into quarters. If feeling extravagant use quails' eggs. As a change mix crisply fried crunchy bacon into the potato or season with freshly chopped herbs.

FILLED PITTA BREADS

Mini-pittas are probably best as the large ones need two hands. Flash the pittas under a hot grill for 1 minute or so, then insert a sharp-pointed knife and make a pocket.

Fillings

1 Cream cheese, chopped olives, pine kernels

2 Curried egg, grated Cheddar, chopped spring onions

3 Cream cheese, finely chopped watercress and chopped walnuts

4 Liver sausage, sliced onion, tomato, crunchy bacon

SAMOSAS

My friend Shamin runs the shop in our village. She makes the most wonderful samosas and showed me how to do it. The pastry dries out very easily so you have to work at the speed of light.

---

8 oz/225 g mince (beef, lamb, pork, veal
or poultry)
2 oz/50 g very finely chopped onion
1 clove garlic very finely chopped
(optional)
1 tablespoon cooked peas
½ teaspoon white cumin seeds
6 crushed coriander seeds
½ teaspoon mixed herbs

½ teaspoon hot chilli powder
Salt and pepper
1 dessertspoon oil

Samosa Pastry
1 lb/450 g plain flour
6 oz/175 g butter
1 teaspoon salt
¼ pint/150 ml water

Sift flour and salt into Magimix, add butter cut into small pieces and process for 15 seconds or until it resembles fine breadcrumbs. Tip into a large bowl and add water gradually. Knead to a hard dough and cover with a damp tea-towel.

To make the filling, sauté the onions for a few minutes with the cumin and then add the mince and chilli powder. Cook for a further 15 minutes over a low heat. Stir in peas and leave until liquid has evaporated. Finally sprinkle on the salt, pepper and chopped coriander. If using crushed coriander seeds add at the same time as the mince. Cool before using.

Roll the dough out and cut into 12 8-inch (20-cm) circles. It may be easier to divide it into 12 lumps beforehand. Cut each circle in half and cover with a damp tea-towel. Brush the edges of each semi-circle with milk or water. Put a spoonful of filling in each. Fold over and join down the centre to make a cone, add more filling if necessary and fold over the top to make a triangle. Deep fry to a golden brown. Leave the ones waiting to be fried still covered.

CONSTANCE'S GAME PATTIES

Auntie Constance produced these delicious little patties last time I stayed with her. Of course they were a legacy of the redoubtable Sophy, and are an excellent way of using up leftover game or poultry. You could increase the quantities and size if you wished.

8 oz/225 g cooked minced game/poultry
¼ pint/150 ml thick béchamel sauce
1 teaspoon finely chopped parsley
1 teaspoon finely chopped chives/tarragon
Salt and pepper

Pastry

4 oz/100 g plain flour
2 oz/50 g butter
Water
Beaten egg
Fresh breadcrumbs
Oil for frying

Make a stiff paste with the flour, butter and water and roll out thinly. Cut into 4-inch (10-cm) circles.

Combine the minced game/poultry with the sauce and add the herbs. Place a heaped teaspoon of cooled mixture in the centre of each circle. Fold over, seal edges with water, dip in egg and breadcrumbs and deep fry in oil. Can be made in advance to the egg and breadcrumb stage and frozen.

LINDA'S DATE AND HONEY BAR

Another of Linda's specialities. Good for energy on a cold day.

8 oz/225 g dates, stoned and chopped	*4 oz/100 g demerara sugar* 4
3 tablespoons honey	*4 oz/100 g self-raising flour* 6
3 tablespoons lemon juice	*3 oz/75 g porridge oats*
2 tablespoons plain flour	*2 oz/50 g crushed Weetabix*
8 tablespoons water	*or 5 oz/150 g oats* 8
	salt

Butter and line a 7-inch (15-cm) square tin with greaseproof paper. Put dates, lemon juice, honey, plain flour and water in a saucepan and bring to the boil slowly, stirring all the time and simmer for 3-4 minutes. Leave to cool. Mix self-raising flour, sugar, oats and melted butter together and spread half over the base of the tin, pressing down well. Spread the date mixture over the top then finish with the other half of the oat mixture (or the crushed Weetabix). Smooth top, and press evenly. Bake in a pre-heated oven at 375°F/190°C/Gas Mark 5 for 25 minutes. Leave to cool and then cut into bars and remove from tin.

PHEASANT SHOOTING — THE FOUR O'CLOCK FEAST

Here you can let yourself go and wander where you will in the realms of gourmet gastronomy. I shall content myself with setting out a menu from one of the Tower Hill shoots. These were devised because with only 10 acres of ground, the actual shooting only lasted for one and a half to two hours, so if we had a 'Major Disaster' at least our guests, some of whom had come a long way, would have something to take their minds off the lack of birds. We generally had anything up to thirty-five people, and on one occasion forty. You probably won't have as many to feed so you can cut down on the number of pâtés and concentrate on only one hot main dish. Otherwise refer to recipes in the section Pheasant Shooting — Lunch at Home. This is a buffet menu:

MENU

GROUSE PÂTÉ with whisky and juniper berries
DUCK LIVER PÂTÉ with brandy and truffles
PARTRIDGE LIVER PÂTÉ paprika
SMOKED PIGEON PÂTÉ with vermouth and honey
TROUT PÂTÉ with almonds
★
TERRINE OF PIGEON with sloe gin
TERRINE OF MALLARD with Madeira and orange
★
SPINACH MOUSSE with cheese and hard-boiled egg
★
CHICORY, ORANGE AND JUNIPER SALAD
CELERIAC REMOULADE
TOMATO RING
FENNEL IN PERNOD SAUCE
RADICCIO AND LETTUCE SALAD
★
OXTAIL STEW
'SHOOTABLE STAG' OR DEVILLED KIDNEYS
★
MASHED POTATOES
★
CHOCCY POTS
ELDERBERRY MOUSSE
TANGERINE SORBET
★
CHEESE & BISCUITS

COFFEE   17.X11.87

73

As you can see, this was quite a tall order even for someone leading what I would call a 'normal' life, that is, with a 'nine-to-five husband'. Archie and I were game-dealers so sod's law was in permanent operation and I could be sure that just as I had set aside a day to make the pâtés there would be a call from one of the shoots to say that they wanted some 'oven-ready' birds for the directors. Only one of our 'ladies' did the drawing so if she was ill I had to stand-in. Panic stations would ensue, as there would be thawed-out packages of livers, pigeon breasts *et al.* all over the kitchen. Latterly poor Archie was on crutches and so depended on me to put him out in his pigeon hide and fetch him in the afternoon. You could bet your bottom dollar that on my one free day there would be a call from a farmer to say 'there are hundreds of pigeons on the rape', so bang would go my schedule. This meant that everything had to be planned very much in advance and I generally chose a menu which contained freezable dishes. With the exception of the salads everything in the above menu can be frozen, though personally I think terrines and mousses are best freshly made and chilled.

I would start planning at least one month in advance and any hole in my diary would be quickly seized upon, and I would try make one or two of the pâtés at a time. A week before the shoot I would consult the oracle and buy the drinks after a discussion of the menu. Inevitably, when we came to puddings Archie always insisted on his favourite Choccy Pots or mousse. Four or five days before the actual shoot, time had to be made for the construction, cooking, weighting and chilling of the terrines. A maximum of two days had to be allowed for the confection of any mousses. A visit to stock up on salad ingredients had to be fitted in, and contingency plans for substitutes made if what you had set your heart on was not available. The day before there were glasses to be arranged, cutlery found (some of which had to be borrowed), and plates and dishes laid out on clean tablecloths. Flowers had to be arranged, beds made up, and if necessary camp beds set up for any unscheduled pre-shoot overnight guests. At lunchtime the day before all items were taken out of the freezer to thaw out, and the various salad dressings and mayonnaise made and put into screw-top jars. At teatime Archie used to sit at the kitchen table with a preserving pan, jars of tomato juice, vodka, and all his secret ingredients. This always seemed to coincide with some delicate culinary operation; nevertheless, everything had to be dropped as he always needed acolytes and tasters. If you weren't very careful you got pretty sloshed before supper had even been thought of.

On top of all this a simple supper had to be dreamed up and made, and a succession of breakfast shifts arranged for the great day. As soon as it was light Archie and Will Garfit would sally forth in the Land-Rover to put out polythene bags as 'stops' and to blank in certain hedgerows. On one never to be forgotten occasion, both Will and Tom Gullick were in the dawn team. There was a thick fog and they got lost (or so they said) and blanked in all the ground from the motorway to Tower Hill — that day we had a record bag! The dawn team were generally home by 8.30, so I left breakfast on the hot-plate and sallied forth in my 'gamekeeper's hat' to feed the pheasants. Before this I had arranged the salads, peeled the potatoes and placed my huge Elizabeth David gallon casserole in the oven on very low. By this time some over-punctual guests had started arriving and had to be offered coffee — more washing-up. Finally at 10.30 all were assembled and The Master gave his talk. No matter that we had all heard it before, he was convinced that we were all idiots and wouldn't know what to do. Between 12 and 12.30 all would be over, and the day judged either a success or a Major Disaster. I was spared any further duties and scuttled home to change, ready to appear as the perfect (sic) hostess. I usually found some non-participant wives hanging about so they were commandeered to hand round drinks, in particular Archie's explosive Bloody Mary. The Guns began to trickle in and gradually a low hum would become a roar of shooting chit-chat. Wonderful Gladys had cooked and mashed the potatoes whilst we were out and at a given signal would begin to put French bread in the oven. Finally the word would be given and everyone fell to. It didn't seem to matter that our house was very small. As many little tables as possible had been set up and furniture moved round. The oldies generally managed to snaffle a place at a table, the others just sat on the floor or the stairs. Archie held court and gradually, replete and satisfied, the guests departed. A few stayed on, and the talk might range from Archie's days in Cairo during the war, when he took part in the Ambassadorial duck shoot, to pre-war fishing exploits — and, of course, any current pigeon shooting exploits.

I don't suggest that you try anything quite so ambitious, but do have a go at a modest gastronomic feast.

DUCK LIVER PÂTÉ

As game dealers we were lucky enough to have all kinds of livers. You can use any wild duck livers that you have saved up in the freezer and make up the difference with turkey or chicken livers.

---

8 oz/225 g duck/chicken livers	*1 truffle + juice from jar or 1 oz/25 g dried*
4 oz/100 g butter	*wild mushrooms soaked for 10 minutes in a*
1 teaspoon redcurrant jelly	*little water then simmered for 20 minutes*
2 tablespoons brandy	*Salt and black pepper*

Serves 4-6

Trim the livers and cut up roughly. Heat butter in a thick pan until foaming. Sauté livers until firm but still faintly pink inside, then pour in the warmed brandy and light. When the flames have died down transfer the livers to the Magimix. Add the truffle juice or the wild mushrooms and their liquid, redcurrant jelly and seasoning, to the pan, and bubble for a few seconds. Process the livers and when finely ground add the liquid. Transfer to a bowl and fold in the finely sliced truffles, reserving a few slices for decoration. Spoon into a dish and lay the remaining truffle slices down the centre. Cool and cover with a thin layer of clarified butter. Refrigerate for a couple of days to develop flavour, then use or freeze.

GROUSE PÂTÉ WITH WHISKY AND JUNIPER BERRIES

This is a quick way of making grouse pâté and is my favourite as it really tastes of grouse. Use old birds, they are cheaper, larger and have more flavour. Large supermarkets sell them in season, or try and find some at your local game dealer.

1 old grouse, raw	*1 teaspoon rowan jelly*
2 oz/50 g butter	*3 fl oz/60 ml whisky*
2 rashers fat bacon	*6 crushed juniper berries*
2 oz/50 g bacon fat or pork lard	*Salt and ground black pepper*

Serves 2-4

Cut off the grouse breasts, sprinkle with juniper berries, pour over the whisky and leave whilst you make stock. Place the carcass in a pan with a carrot, onion, leek and some mixed herbs and cover with water. Simmer until reduced to ¼ pint (150ml). Remove the breasts, dry well and cut into dice. Sauté together with the bacon in the butter and bacon fat until just pink. Remove to the Magimix and process until really finely ground. To the pan juices add the whisky, rowan jelly, stock and seasoning. Bubble until the liquid has almost disappeared then pour into the Magimix and blend again. Pour into pots and decorate with bay leaves and whole juniper berries covered with aspic. If you are going to freeze the pâté do this when it has thawed out.

PARTRIDGE/CHICKEN LIVER PÂTÉ PAPRIKA

This was a very gourmet recipe I dreamed up when we were game-dealers as we had so many surplus partridge livers. It is nearly as good made with chicken livers but if you should have any partridges, do hoard them. I hate to tell you that it took the livers from 20 birds to make 8 oz (225 g).

8 oz/225 g partridge/chicken livers or mixture of both	*1 heaped teaspoon paprika*
4 oz/100 g unsalted butter	*3 fl oz/60 ml brandy*
1 shallot, finely chopped	*½ teaspoon basil or oregano*
¼ pint/150 ml thick double cream or fromage frais	*½ crushed clove garlic (optional)*
	Salt and freshly ground pepper

Serves 4-6

Trim the livers and chop coarsely. Melt butter until foaming and sauté livers and shallot. Livers should still be faintly pink. Remove to Magimix. Add brandy, cream, paprika, herbs and seasoning to pan and bubble for a few seconds. Add to puréed livers and blend until really smooth. Pour into pots and, when cold, pour over clarified butter. Decorate with bay leaves and a pinch of paprika. Chill or freeze.

SMOKED PIGEON PÂTÉ

This is one of my creations which everyone seems to like, but it does need a trout smoker. If you don't own or can't borrow one, adapt the recipe by just sautéeing the pigeon breasts (but do them until faintly pink), use all the ingredients and follow the instructions except the smoking, and you will then have an unusual pigeon pâté.

---

8 pigeon breasts (4 pigeons)	1 teaspoon stem ginger juice or dry ground
5 rashers of streaky bacon	ginger
3 oz/75 g shallot, finely chopped	1 tablespoon cream
4 oz/100 g unsalted butter	¼ teaspoon ground cloves
4 fl oz/100 ml vermouth	½ teaspoon mild Dijon mustard
1 teaspoon runny honey	1 pinch dill weed
2 teaspoons lemon juice	Salt and ground black pepper to taste

---

Serves 4–6

Sprinkle 1½ tablespoons sawdust over the bottom of the smoker, put in the grid and drip tray. Lay pigeon breasts on the grid and cover with 3 of the bacon rashers. Slide on the lid and put the smoke box over the lighted methylated spirits container and leave until flames have died out. Sauté shallots and remaining rashers in the butter until transparent then add the pigeon breasts cut into 1-inch (2½-cm) pieces and sauté for a few seconds. Fish out and put into Magimix and process until finely ground. Pour the juice from the drip tray into the sauté pan together with the rest of the ingredients. Bubble for a few minutes and then add to the ground pigeon. Blend until really smooth and creamy, then pour into pots, cover with melted butter and chill for 2–3 days. Freezes well. Serve at room temperature, and not straight out of the fridge or it will not spread well.

SMOKED TROUT PÂTÉ WITH ALMONDS

A good way of using up those rather tasteless stillwater rainbows or, if no one in the family fishes, smoked trout is easily obtainable from your fishmonger or from supermarkets.

8 oz/225 g smoked trout, skinned and boned	*1 oz/25 g flaked almonds*
4 oz/100 g butter	*1 dessertspoon finely chopped parsley*
1/8 pint/75 ml double cream	*Lemon juice*
	Salt and pepper

Serves 2-4

Fry the almonds in the butter until golden, then remove to a dish. Process the trout with the cream and pour in half the butter through the top of the Magimix. Add lemon juice, salt and pepper and the parsley. Pour into a bowl and stir in half the almonds which you have slightly chopped. Spoon into a china dish and allow to get firm in the fridge. Finally pour over the rest of the butter and decorate with the remaining almonds, which should be whole. The crunchy texture of the almonds makes this a bit out of the ordinary.

TERRINE OF PIGEON WITH SLOE GIN

I find pâté-lovers divide into 'smoothies' and 'roughies'. This will please pigeon aficionados who like something of a coarser texture than the Smoked Pigeon Pâté.

10 pigeon breasts (5 pigeons)	*2 fl oz/60 ml sloe gin*
4 oz/100 g pig's liver	*1/2 teaspoon dried thyme*
4 oz/100 g minced pork	*1/4 teaspoon ground cloves*
4 oz/100 g pork fat minced or coarsely chopped	*1 thick slice white bread, crusts cut off*
8 rashers smoked streaky bacon	*1 egg beaten up in 2 fl oz/60 ml milk*
2 shallots, finely chopped	*Bay leaves to decorate*
	Salt and plenty of ground black pepper

Serves 6-8

Pull the fillets away from the underside of the breasts and lay in a dish, pour over sloe gin and leave for 2 hours. Chop or mince the liver, the pigeon breasts (use carcasses for stock), and 2 of the rashers. Mix together with the bread slice soaked in egg and milk, pork, pork fat, shallots, marinade liquor, herbs and seasoning. Line an earthenware terrine with 6 rashers flattened with the back of a knife. Spoon in half the mixture, lay the fillets on top and cover with the rest of the mixture. Decorate top with remaining rashers and bay leaves. Cover tightly with foil and lid and stand in a baking dish of boiling water. Cook in a pre-heated oven at 350°F/175°C/Gas Mark 4 for 2 hours or until juice runs clear when you stick in a skewer. Remove from oven, place a 2 lb (900 g) weight on top and when cool place in fridge for 2-3 days to allow flavours to develop. If to be frozen be more liberal with the seasonings as freezing dissipates the flavour of salt and pepper.

TERRINE OF MALLARD WITH ORANGE AND MADEIRA

This excellent recipe was given to me by a friend whose family live in the Sologne, France's best-known district for game and, in particular, duck. This is a very spectacular dish and if you are only going to have one terrine for your buffet you can double the quantity.

---

1 uncooked mallard	*3 fl oz/80 ml Madeira*
4 oz/100 g pork fat	*¼ teaspoon ground mace*
4 oz/100 g lean pork	*Salt and pepper*
2 shallots finely chopped	*6 oz/175 g pork flare fat or hard back fat*
1 egg, well beaten	*to line terrine*
Juice of 1 orange	*½ pint/275 ml aspic jelly made with 3*
Zest of 1 orange	*heaped teaspoons dissolved in*
½ teaspoon dried thyme	*½ pint/275 ml boiling water*

Serves 4-6

Remove breasts from duck and slice very thinly lengthways. Marinade in orange juice and Madeira for 2 hours. Remove rest of duck flesh and mince with lean and fat pork, then mix with beaten egg, seasoning and marinade liquor. Line bottom and sides of small terrine with thin strips of flare or back fat. Fill with alternate layers of mince and fillets, starting and ending with mince. Cover tightly and cook in a roasting dish filled with boiling water in a pre-heated oven at 350°F/175°C/Gas Mark 4 for 1½ hours, or until juice runs clear. Press under a weight and when cool refrigerate. Remove any specks of fat which have come to the surface. Pour over a layer of aspic and when set lay very thin slices of orange down the centre, slightly overlapping, then pour over a final layer of aspic. If to be frozen do this when unthawed.

SPINACH MOUSSE WITH CHEESE AND HARD-BOILED EGG

This is another colourful buffet dish and you can mix and match all sorts of ingredients with the spinach. By the way, if using hard-boiled eggs, don't freeeze as the chopped whites turn a nasty grey.

1 x 8 oz/225 g packet frozen chopped spinach, unthawed
3 eggs
¼ pint/150 ml milk
Bay leaf, onion ring, pinch mixed herbs, 6 peppercorns, salt, small piece garlic (optional)
4 oz/100 g grated strong Cheddar cheese
2 shallots, finely chopped
1 oz/50 g butter

¼ pint/150 ml thick béchamel sauce
1 pinch oregano
1 pinch nutmeg
2 tablespoons Hellman's mayonnaise
½ pint/275 ml cream, whipped
2 hard-boiled eggs, coarsely chopped
1½ pkts gelatine dissolved in 1 tablespoon water
Salt, pepper and cayenne

Serves 6-8

Thaw the spinach and drain well. Sauté the shallots in the butter until cooked, add the spinach, béchamel sauce, oregano and nutmeg. Heat through. Make a custard with the milk, egg yolks and seasonings in a small bowl over hot water. Strain and add to spinach together with cheese, hard-boiled eggs, and melted gelatine. When cool fold in whipped cream and mayonnaise. When just beginning to set add the stiffly beaten whites of egg. Cover with cling-film and chill.

SALADS

CHICORY, ORANGE AND JUNIPER SALAD

This goes very well with roast duck.

4 heads chicory	1 teaspoon crushed juniper berries
1 orange peeled and then sliced in rings	1/4 pint/150 ml olive oil
1/2 orange squeezed	Salt and ground black pepper
1 teaspoon wine vinegar	

Slice the chicory in rings, as it's then easier to eat with a fork. Add the sliced orange and at the last minute pour over the dressing made from the rest of the ingredients.

CELERIAC REMOULADE

It is very important to use *mild* Dijon mustard for the sauce. A friend of mine who had tried the recipe from my other cookbook, *Prue's Country Kitchen*, complained that it was very bitter. When 'grilled' by me it transpired that she'd just used ordinary French mustard — fatal!

1 large or 2 medium celeriac	1 tablespoon white wine vinegar
4 tablespoons mild Dijon mustard	1 tablespoon cream
3 tablespoons boiling water	Salt and pepper
1/4-1/2 pint/150-175 ml olive oil	

Peel celeriac and cut in julienne strips; I use the Alumette potato disc of the Magimix. Plunge into boiling salted water and when it re-boils pour into a colander and run under the cold tap. Drain well and pat with a clean tea-towel. Warm Magimix bowl, put in mustard, switch on, add boiling water drop by drop, and then the oil as for mayonnaise. Finally add vinegar, salt, pepper and cream. Mix into celeriac. Best made overnight.

TOMATO RING

This makes a good blodge of colour on your buffet and is an alternative to tomato salad.

2 x 14 oz/395 g tins peeled tomatoes	2 finely chopped spring onions
2½ pkts aspic	1 teaspoon each chopped chives, parsley,
1 x 4 oz/100 g carton cottage cheese	basil
1 dessertspoon demerara sugar	¼ teaspoon each garlic and lemon pepper
2 fl oz/60 ml sherry	1 teaspoon salt

Process tinned tomatoes slightly, so that they are still lumpy. Bring ½ pint (275 ml) tomato purée and the sherry to the boil and melt the aspic in it. Break the cottage cheese up with a fork and add the aspic and all the other ingredients to the tomato. Pour into a wetted 1½-pint (850-ml) ring mould. Turn out just before serving and fill with cold cooked peas.

FENNEL IN PERNOD SAUCE

Site this near your fish pâté, as they go very well together.

2 bulbs fennel	1 dessertspoon olive oil
2 fl oz/60 ml Pernod	Salt and pepper
1 teaspoon lemon juice	

Remove coarse outer leaves and slice fennel bulbs very finely into rings. Mix together with the other ingredients.

RADICCIO AND LETTUCE SALAD

Make an ordinary salad with radiccio and lettuce of your choice. Failing radiccio, substitute lollo rosso. Dress with Archie's Dressing (see p.15).

MAIN COURSES

OXTAIL STEW

Follow the recipe for Salmi of Oxtail and Wild Duck in the section Pheasant Shooting —
Lunch at Home (p.44-5), but omit the duck.

'SHOOTABLE STAG' OR DEVILLED KIDNEYS

Like Choccy Pots (see below) Archie always insisted that this should be included in any
menu. Its rather misleading name denoted the extremely pretty girl who gave the recipe to
Archie on one of his lecture tours.

---

12 lamb's kidneys, skinned and trimmed	*English mustard and lemon juice*
1 dessertspoon Worcester Sauce	*1 dessertspoon flour*
3 oz/75 g butter	*1 dessertspoon tomato ketchup*
1 teaspoon each of curry powder, made	*Salt and cayenne pepper*

Serves 4-6

Roll the kidneys in the flour, salt and cayenne. Heat butter and lemon juice over a low flame
and tip in the kidneys. Add all the other ingredients and cook very slowly until done but
still pink in the middle. Can be made the day before and re-heated very slowly. You can
serve a dish of Prue's Perfect Rice (pp.39-40) with it if you like.

PUDDINGS

CHOCCY POTS

At last we come to Archie's favourite pudding. It is very easy to make and freezes well. It
thaws out at room temperature in about an hour or so, which is useful if disaster strikes and
you are suddenly landed with unexpected guests.

8 oz/225 g Bitter Menier chocolate	4 eggs
2 heaped teaspoons instant coffee dissolved in 1 dessertspoon water	1 dessertspoon brandy or liqueur of your choice.
1 oz/25 g unsalted butter	

Serves 8

Break up chocolate and melt in a basin over hot water together with the coffee and liqueur. Break in egg yolks one by one and stir well. Then add the butter cut into tiny cubes. Beat until mixture looks shiny. Remove from hot water and allow to cool. Pour into a larger bowl and fold in the stiffly beaten whites of egg. Spoon into pots, ramekins or glasses and chill. This serves 8 but you can increase the quantity. It is worked out on the basis of 2 oz (50 g) chocolate to 1 egg.

ELDERBERRY MOUSSE

This presupposes that you have been inattentive during partridge drives earlier in the season and have picked elderberries into a plastic bag instead of marking your husband's birds. Substitute blackberries if necessary.

1½ lbs/675 g elderberries	¼ pint/150 ml double cream
4 oz/100 g sugar	1 pkt gelatine
3 eggs	1 tablespoon water

Serves 6-8

Cook elderberries over a low heat with the sugar until soft. Pour into Magimix and process until smooth. Press through a nylon strainer to remove pips, and re-heat. Put back into Magimix and switch on. Remove pusher and break in egg yolks one by one, then add gelatine dissolved in water. Pour into bowl and allow to cool, then fold in cream whipped to soft peaks. When mixture just begins to set fold in stiffly beaten whites of egg and refrigerate.

TANGERINE SORBET

You should always have a stock of these in your freezer as they are both delicious and, when piled up into a glass dish, really look terrific. Try and get real tangerines, the flavour is better and it's easier to winkle out the insides.

12 tangerines
Juice of 2 lemons
8 oz/275 g lump sugar
½ pint/275 ml fruit juice (tangerine and

lemon)
1 pint/575 ml water
2 egg whites, stiffly beaten.

Serves 12

IN BETWEEN DRIVES

Cut 2 inches (4½ cm) round from top of tangerines and ease out flesh with a teaspoon. Place on a flat baking sheet and freeze. Process flesh in Magimix and then press through a nylon strainer. Add lemon juice and make up to ½ pint (275 ml) with more juice. Bring water and sugar slowly to boil, stirring to dissolve sugar, then boil fast for 5 minutes. Allow to cool and then add to fruit juice. Pour into a bowl and place in coldest part of freezer. Stir every half hour until it is the consistency of very thick mayonnaise. Add stiffly beaten egg whites and stir well. Leave for half an hour and then beat with electric beaters. Leave for 10 minutes and then spoon into tangerine cases. Place hats on top and stick in a bay leaf. To serve, pile in a pyramid in a glass or white china bowl or dish. Take out of freezer 15 minutes before serving.

PHEASANT SHOOTING — MID-MORNING SNACKS AND DRINKS TO STAVE OFF HUNGER BEFORE SITTING DOWN TO THE FOUR O'CLOCK FEAST

Snipe

At about mid-day I am always starving if it is a 'shoot-straight-through' kind of day, and always look forward to the 'twelveses'. One of the nicest breaks was at Will Garfit's Hauxton shoot last season, where as pre-snack drinks we had sherry glasses of champagne. Just enough to pep us up. If the shoot is adjacent to your house it is nice if the snacks can be brought out hot from the oven, but if not plenty of foil and an insulated bag will do wonders. Don't forget small glasses or metal cups for the alcoholic 'nips' and a bottle of sherry or vodka for the soup.

SNACKS

Tiny sausage rolls, streaky rashers rolled up and cooked on a skewer, cheese biscuits, hot chipolatas, tiny balls of sausage meat, scotch eggs made with quail's eggs and, if the weather is not too cold, small smoked salmon or pâté sandwiches. They need to be rather on the lines of hot cocktail canapés — not too substantial as you are going to have a pretty good tuck-in later on.

SOUPS

These should not be too filling, and as most people pour in a good slosh of alcohol a consommé is preferable. I like a really strong, well-flavoured game, chicken or meat stock as a basis. It doesn't matter what you throw into the pot, carcasses of pigeon, pheasant, partridge, chicken or bones of venison. Cover with water and add carrots, onion stuck with cloves, leek, celery, herbs, redcurrant jelly, salt and pepper. Cook for several hours and then strain. I keep all the plastic dishes from meat bought at Sainsbury's into which I pour the stock when cool, and then freeze. At the appointed time I take out one or two, heat up and perhaps add a stock cube if it tastes 'thin'. If you are feeling lazy just use tinned consommé, there are several different varieties. Best of all on a really cold day is a hot Bullshot.

HOT BULLSHOT

---

2 cartons tomato juice	*½ teaspoon celery salt*
2 tins beef consommé	*Worcester Sauce to taste*
1 dessertspoon demerara sugar	*Tabasco sauce to taste*
1 squeeze lemon juice	*Sloshes of vodka to taste — be generous!*
1 teaspoon oregano	

Serves 10-12

Mix the tomato juice and consommé and heat gently but do not boil. Add the seasonings and lastly the vodka. It is very warming.

PRUE'S PUNCH

This is what I serve to the carol singers when they call in here, as well as on shoot days. I have cut down the more alcoholic ingredients in deference to the afternoon's shooting, as when the 'Ladies' leave Tower Hill and hit the cold night air some are not quite so steady on their legs as they might be, and a great deal of giggling is to be heard, especially from Gladys. Heat up in a large saucepan — but do not boil — the following:

2 bottles red 'plonk'	1 apple stuck with cloves
1 wine glass brandy	¼ teaspoon freshly grated nutmeg (or
Juice of 2 lemons	powdered)
Juice of 2 oranges	Sugar to taste
1 stick cinnamon	

Serves 10-12

When thoroughly hot leave to steep for 10 minutes then strain and pour into a heated thermos flask. Can be made the day before and then re-heated, but *do not allow to boil.*

SLOE GIN

This is the basic recipe for any of the plum family. Vodka is just as good if you don't like gin. My best *vendange* was some years ago when Archie was pigeon shooting on the then Rank Estate, where there were towering strips of wild plums planted by Lord Rank to fly partridges over. The fruit came in all colours, burgundy, ruby, amber and, when ripe, had fallen in profusion and fermented — one day I actually saw a cock pheasant which was drunk. Bullaces, sloes, garden plums or damsons are all good. You don't need to prick them, just put in the freezer and when you have thawed them out they will split and save you the trouble.

5 lbs/2.2 kg fruit of your choice	3-4 drops almond essence (optional)
1½ lbs/675 g lump sugar	1 bottle gin, vodka or brandy

Put the split or pricked fruit into a clean plastic or glass sweet jar, add the sugar and top up with your favoured liquor. Cover tightly and place in a dark cupboard. Shake occasionally to dissolve sugar. Leave for at least two months, then strain into clean bottles.

BREACH ORANGE VODKA

We used to slurp this down at a dear neighbour's after lunch. It was so good that all of us drank far more than was good for us, and I feel if there had been a drink/shooting test as opposed to a drink/driving test none of us would have passed. These friends have now moved north, so Scotland beware! The recipe I was given specified 1 gallon of vodka so I have cut it down to half, which makes 3 bottles.

½ gallon (refuse to go metric here) vodka	*4 lemons*
4 Seville oranges	*1½ lbs/675 g lump sugar*

Peel the oranges and lemons very thinly, taking care not to leave any pith on the peel. Stick the rinds into a ½-gallon glass jar (the kind you buy at Boots for making wine). Add the sugar and vodka and cork tightly. Leave for at least three months in a dark cupboard and shake occasionally to dissolve the sugar, then strain and pour into clean bottles.

LUCY'S RASPBERRY VODKA

2 punnets raspberries
1 bottle vodka

8 oz/225 g lump sugar

Put the raspberries into screwtop jar or bottle large enough to take all the ingredients. If it is too small the principle of Archimedes will apply and the juice will overflow. Stopper tightly and place in a dark cupboard. Turn upside down gently every so often. After two months strain and bottle. Add more sugar if it is too tart. Use the raspberries for an alcoholic ice cream or mousse.

WILDFOWLING

Canadian Geese

Never having personally sampled the joys of getting up at crack of or pre-dawn to wade out in slimy mud, sit in the freezing cold, probably slip into a gully and get soaked, I don't actually know what it's like to go wildfowling. From masochistic friends who do so I am told that excitement and the early hour preclude any pangs of hunger, so I can only offer two liquid suggestions, both of which can be made overnight and put in a warmed thermos.

TOM'S TIPPLE

Before joining 'Cappy', short for Capitano, the chief beater in Spain, the only breakfast that Tom can face is a large glass of *caffe con leche*, very sweet white coffee made with masses of sweetened condensed milk with a severe shot of 103 Spanish brandy. This is guaranteed to arm you against any disaster, Major or Minor. It is often freezingly cold in the mountains where we shoot with Tom, so much so that loaders often make a fire in the butt. The first time he saw this Archie nearly did his nut, but the fires were dowsed when the beat started and the partridges seemed quite unaffected.

RALPH'S RUM

Ralph, an old friend now sadly no longer with us, was a fantastic shot and a dedicated sportsman. His fight-the-cold potion comprised hot milk generously laced with rum.

My suggestion is that on returning from the morning flight the weary wildfowler should

94

eat a seriously calorific and cholesterol-ridden 'brunch'. Before going out on his evening flight he can stoke up on a variation of the brunch, ie High Tea, but with the addition of scones, cake, lardy cake or the like. This was one of Archie's favourite meals, and when we went to Scotland we always made a point of staying at a B & B so that he could indulge. It was always 'nip and tuck' as to whether we actually found one before night fell, as the rules of the game demanded that you should never book in advance.

WILDFOWLER'S BRUNCH or HIGH TEA

Menu I

2 fried eggs
Fried bacon
Fried sausage, black pudding or white pudding
Fried tomatoes
2 oatcakes scrumbled up and fried in the fat
Fried bread

Menu II

Scrambled eggs on a thick piece of toast
Kipper fillets
Drop scones, toast and blackberry jelly

Menu III

2 fried eggs
Fried bacon
Waffles (supermarkets have them), heated and covered in plenty of maple syrup
Fried tomatoes

Menu IV

2 fried eggs
2 slices lightly fried ham
Fried mushrooms
Fried potato cakes

Menu V

Fried liver, bacon and potatoes

Menu VI

Baked beans
Poached egg
Fried bacon and sausage or rounds of Cumberland sausage

If the wildfowlers are cooking for themselves then I do not imagine that their wives will have accompanied them, so that is why I have reduced the required culinary expertise to mostly frying! Such things as cakes, scones or the like they can take with them, and plenty of bread, butter, jam and cheese, as well as lots of chocolate/snacks/biscuits.

PIGEON SHOOTING

After over three decades of being married to Archie you would have thought that I must be the definitive expert on what to give the professional or putative pigeon shooter. You would be wrong. Frequently I would send him out with a particularly delectable lunch box, only to find on his return that it was untouched because he had not had time to eat it as there had been so much shooting. At other times it would come back empty because he had dropped it whilst a particulary tricky pigeon came in and the dog had scoffed the lot. Otherwise just as I had cooked a gastronomic supper he would say he wasn't hungry because he had only just finished his sandwiches. If the weather was cold he would complain that there wasn't enough to eat, and if hot that he wasn't hungry. I just went plugging on, and sometimes I got it right.

THE LONG DAY-OUT IN WINTER

The best kind of container for a pigeon-shooter's lunch is a plastic Tupperware sandwich box with divider, or a similar kind of freezer container. A stainless steel Aladdin thermos is almost obligatory as the ordinary kind almost always gets dropped and broken. To cut down on clobber Archie used just to have one filled with tea because he liked at the end of a cold day to have a 'hot cinder' — a cup of tea with a good slosh of whisky in it. For guests I always provided soup, tea or coffee.

LUNCH BOXES

Menu I

COLD CURRIED MINCE and CHUTNEY in a large bap
CREAM CHEESE and APPLE JELLY sandwiched between white bread
1 bar chocolate

Menu II

HAM, EMMENTHAL CHEESE, SLICED TOMATO and CHOPPED
SPRING ONIONS in a large pitta bread
STUFFED EGG made with 1 hard-boiled egg halved and mashed with mayonnaise,
chopped cress or watercress, salt and pepper

Menu III

SARDINE SPECIAL, made with sardines mashed up with chopped spring onion,
mixed herbs, Worcester Sauce, tomato ketchup and pinch of curry powder in a brown bap
or 'hoagy'
CREAM CHEESE, LIVER PÂTÉ and CRISPY BACON, in a sandwich
1 sandwich filled with APRICOT/NUT SPREAD. Chop up 1 cup of dried apricot
in Magimix. Put in a saucepan with ¼ cup brown sugar and ½ cup orange juice and
cook for 30 minutes. Stir in 2 tablespoons finely chopped walnuts and 1 dessertspoon
currants. Cool and refrigerate. Spread on granary or rye bread.

No pigeon shooter's lunch would be complete without one of Archie's favourite's. He
frequently used to speak of his time in the Southern Sudan during the war. His cookboy,
Ishimael, used to dig the groundnuts, peel them, roast them slightly, rub off the skin and
then crush them with a rolling pin made from a bottle. Many and varied were the dishes
concoted by Ishimael which were enhanced by peanuts — 'Gadaddiwaddy' or guineafowl
in a peanut sauce and, in particular, peanut butter soup. Lucy and I obstinately refused to
make this as we thought it sounded so revolting, but on Archie's seventieth birthday party
we made it as a surprise and I have to say it was really delicious. I give the recipe later on

and if you are brave enough to try it you will be amazed at how good it is; don't tell your guests — they will never guess. Lucy brought back some excellent peanut butter combinations from America which make interesting sandwiches.

Menu IV

CRUNCHY PEANUT BUTTER, GRATED CARROT, CRUNCHY BACON and MAYONNAISE or PEANUT BUTTER, GRATED CARROT, RAISINS AND ORANGE JUICE whizzed in the Magimix
1 ONION and MUSTARD sandwich made with bread spread with mayonnaise and French mustard and filled with very thin rings of Spanish or sweet red onion
1 CHOCOLATE ROLL. Slice of very new white bread, crusts cut off, generously spread with cream cheese or butter and sprinkled with chocolate drops or buttons, and then rolled up and wrapped in foil or cling-film

---

Menu V

---

1 or 2 sausage rolls
1 CHEESE AND BEER SPREAD sandwich. 4oz/50 g grated cheddar, 2 fl oz/60 ml beer, dash tabasco and Worcester Sauce blended to a spreading consistency with butter
1 piece Gingerbread (see below)

JENNY GAY'S GINGERBREAD

Jenny used to pick our *fraises des bois* and, one never-to-be forgotten year, we grew new potatoes in partnership together, and made enough from the sale of them to buy ourselves each a new evening dress. She comes from Newcastle and has a fund of the most marvellous North Country recipes, some of which she has given me. The following is one of them.

8 oz/225 g self-raising flour	2 oz/50 g soft brown sugar (muscovado for
½ teaspoon salt	preference)
1 teaspoon ground ginger	4 oz/100 g golden syrup or black treacle
3 oz/75 g raisins, sultanas or 2 oz/50 g	or ½ and ½
chopped stem or crystallised ginger	1 egg beaten up in milk to make ¼
2 oz/50 g butter or margarine	pint/150 ml

Mix together flour, salt, ginger and chosen fruit in bowl. Melt butter/margarine, sugar and syrup in pan and add to flour with egg and milk. Mix well. Pour into greased square 7-in (15-cm) tin and bake in pre-heated oven at 350°F/175°C/Gas Mark 4 for 45 minutes. Cool, then cut in squares.

Menu VI

2 BAKED BEAN, BACON and CHEESE sandwiches. Mash together the baked beans, scrunched crispy bacon and spread between granary bread with thinly sliced cheese
1 CREAM CHEESE, JELLY and WATERCRESS roll

Tom is inordinately fond of baked beans, and when I worked for him in the travel business I would call in at his flat with papers, hoping to find something in the kitchen to eat, but there was never anything except baked beans. The only concession to variety that he made was to curry them. When I produced this he thought it was the bee's knees.

SOUPS

Any of the soups previously mentioned would be suitable, but here are one or two more suggestions.

PUMPKIN AND TOMATO SOUP

Archie's passion for pumpkin soup went to extraordinary lengths. Once we were bidden to arrive at a shoot at nine in the morning. Not having been before Archie did not want to be late, and as we had to take our very ancient Land-Rover we allowed far too much time and arrived at eight o'clock. The keeper kindly invited us in to have a coffee, and out of the window we could see six amazing pumpkins, each big enough for Cinderella's coach, the largest of which had been entered for a pumpkin competition. Archie instantly went into overdrive and a deal was struck there and then. After shooting the biggest was loaded into the back of the Land-Rover. It was so heavy I couldn't lift it out unaided and it took two days and several preserving pans to get it all cooked and frozen.

---

8 oz/225 g diced raw pumpkin
1 onion, finely chopped
4 oz/100 g tomato peeled, de-seeded and chopped
1 garlic clove, finely chopped
¼ teaspoon freshly grated nutmeg

1 heaped teaspoon demerara sugar
1 tablespoon oil
½ pint/275 ml chicken stock (or stock cube and water)
½ pint/275 ml milk
Salt and pepper

Serves 2

Cook the pumpkin, tomato, onion and garlic in the oil over a very low heat in a covered pan until transparent, then add the rest of the ingredients and cook for a further 10 to 15 minutes. Pureé in the Magimix until creamy and re-heat.

ISHIMAEL'S PEANUT BUTTER SOUP

2 large tablespoons smooth peanut butter
½ pint/275 ml chicken stock (or stock cube and water)

½ pint/275 ml milk
Salt and plenty of ground black pepper

Serves 2

Bring the stock and milk to the boil. Place the peanut butter in the Magimix, switch on and pour in the liquids and season. Nothing could be simpler and in a matter of minutes you have a really filling and nutritious soup.

PIGEON SHOOTING — SUMMER

THE EVEN LONGER DAY-OUT IN SUMMER

This always used to be a very tiring time of the year for the Professional Pigeon Shooter's wife. The morning was devoted to gardening, typing articles for Archie or doing various keepering jobs. Next, lunch, and then getting the stuff into the Land-Rover ready for the important business of the day. At harvest-time, when it might be hot and thundery, light sandwiches were the order of the day and, most important, in addition to the mandatory thermos of tea would be another of iced *citron presse,* apple juice or the like and a bottle of water (with a bowl) for the dog. Archie, or Archie plus one or two guests if it was a weekend (they would have had to be lunched), would set off. I then gardened or was housewifely. A tempting supper was prepared and the long wait would begin for the returning hunters. At any time between nine and ten they might appear, but this did not mean that we would eat right away, oh, no! First the dog had to be fed, then the pigeons unloaded and the worst chore of all undertaken — the dreaded 'de-flying'. This horrible job meant plucking off the feathers under the wings and pulling off the heads of any pigeons where the blowflies had laid their eggs. Even the strongest men blenched at the thought, and I usually ended up doing it. Sometimes we would sit down to dinner at ten-thirty or eleven, and did not get to bed until after midnight. It really was a long day.

LIGHT LUNCH BOX FARE

Menu I

FETA CHEESE, CHOPPED OLIVES and TOMATOES in a half baguette, split nearly through, seasoned with salt and pepper and best olive oil dribbled over. GRAPES, washed and placed in a Flora container or similar, inside the lunch box

---

Menu II

PRAWNS, CHOPPED FENNEL and MAYONNAISE in a hollowed-out salad bap. PLUMS

Menu III

SHREDDED CABBAGE, CARROT, CHOPPED SPRING ONION, HAM and MAYONNAISE in a large pitta bread. NECTARINE

Menu IV

CHICKEN, MAYONNAISE, ALMONDS, CHOPPED WATERCRESS all mixed together and stuffed into two small baps. ORANGE peeled and quartered and placed in Flora container as above

---

Menu V

CORNED BEEF and HORSERADISH with CREAM CHEESE, DIJON MUSTARD, CHOPPED PARSLEY and MAYONNAISE. Slice corned beef very thinly. Blend rest of ingredients and spread on granary bread. Lay on top a thick layer of corned beef slices, sprinkle on chopped gherkins and sandwich together. PEAR

Menu VI

SMOKED TROUT, HARD-BOILED EGG, FROMAGE FRAIS, SLICED ONION, DILL BUTTER. Fork together the trout, chopped egg and fromage frais. Blend together butter and chopped fresh or dried dill. Spread on pumpernickel bread and fill generously with trout mixture and thinly sliced onion. Wrap in foil or cling-film as pumpernickel tends to curl up at the edges when exposed to the air. BANANA and washed CHERRIES

CITRON PRESSÉ. Squeeze 2 lemons, add 1 pint/575 ml water, ice cubes and sweeten to taste. Pour into chilled thermos with curl of rind.

THE POST 'DE-FLYING' FAMILY PICNIC

My first memory of this gruesome chore was soon after we were married. Archie and I had gone with a friend up to Berkshire, where they had shot 450 pigeons between them. We sat in the middle of a sheep rape field on top of the downs 'de-flying'. The pigeons were then laid out to cool while we had supper, then they had to be brought home, put into hampers and taken to the station to catch the midnight train for Smithfield Market.

The other outstanding occasion took place soon after Archie came out of hospital. We were called to deal with pigeons on three huge rape stubbles. One of our 'First Eleven' was with us, on leave from Northern Ireland, plus his newly acquired, very glamorous blonde American girlfriend and, of all unlikely things, the schoolboy son of a vicar friend. It was one of those sticky, hot, thundery days and by the evening we were dripping. They shot a lot of pigeons. At close of play the Master ordained that the 'de-flying' session should take place. Unfortunately I didn't have a camera — the expression on our guests' faces had to be seen to be believed. They coped manfully and Laura's exquisitely manicured nails picked and plucked with the best, but Lucy reminds me that we drank a great deal of vodka and tonic, so that may have had something to do with it. It has to be said that the gallant soldier looked very sick, and on future occasions I always noticed that he managed to be doing something else when 'de-flying' volunteers were called for.

CHECK LIST FOR THE MID-SUMMER PIGEON PICNIC

Gallon plastic container of water, soap, nailbrush, nailfile, towel and plastic washing-up bowl for hygiene after 'de-flying'

If you really want to earn 'Brownie Points' bring man's hairbrush/comb/eau de cologne or aftershave

Dog food. If using tin best to bring unopened because of flies, and mix with biscuit on site. Bring extra in case any guests have forgotten to bring food for their hound

Extra drinking water for dog(s)/humans

Tin-opener

Bottle-opener

Large heavy-duty plastic bin-bag

1 wide-mouthed thermos filled with ice

1 large thermos filled with cold soft drink of your choice

1 large thermos filled with chilled soup, if it's on your menu

Whisky/vodka/gin or whatever hard liquor you decide on, but Pimm's, chilled wine (you can make a spritzer with soda water) or sangria are far more cooling. However, the older members may need a shot of whisky to revive them

Corkscrew

Cans of beer in a cold-box

Cold-box or bag

Cutlery

Napkins are nice, but not strictly necessary

Plates, china, plastic or paper

Salt, pepper, sugar

Plenty of glasses, plastic or glass, for soup and drinks

Rugs or chairs are unnecessary as you can either sit on the ground or use sacks/coats/camouflage nets

Torch. Very important as before you know where you are darkness has fallen and you can't see to collect all the used picnic items.

THE PIGEON PICNIC

The summer shooting supper should be light and easily eaten. You will have to contend with people who are tired, hot, thirsty, and possibly cross if the pigeons have not co-operated. An efficient bar service is the top priority and once they have quenched their thirst and/or had a 'pick-me-up' things will calm down and you can dish out the supper while they hold a pigeon post-mortem. Not literally, of course; it is much like a bridge post-mortem, when everyone accuses everyone else in the politest possible way of not doing the right thing at the right time, and in the right place. Any pigeon shooter, and in particular Archie's 'First Eleven', will know exactly what I mean.

MENU
SPINACH AND SORREL SOUP
PITTA BREADS
MIXED SALAD AND ARCHIE'S DRESSING
STRAWBERRIES AND CREAM or GREEK YOGURT
ICED MINT AND LEMON TEA

SPINACH AND SORREL SOUP

8 oz/225 g frozen, chopped spinach	½ pint/150 ml water
4 oz/100 g fresh sorrel (a good handful), chopped	½ pint/150 ml milk
	1 dessertspoon sugar
1 shallot, finely chopped	Salt and pepper
1 oz/25 g butter or 1 tablespoon sunflower oil	2 egg yolks
	¹/₈ pint single cream or fromage frais
½ vegetable stock cube	

Serves 4

Sauté the shallot in the butter and oil, then add the spinach and sorrel. Cook gently for 10 minutes then add the stock cube, water and sugar. Simmer for 5 minutes then blend until smooth in the Magimix. Pour back into saucepan, add milk and re-heat, season to taste. Pull off the stove and stir in the egg yolks beaten up in the cream or fromage frais. Cool and refrigerate. Pour into a chilled thermos.

CHAUDFROID OF CHICKEN

4 skinless chicken breasts
½ pint/275 ml good chicken stock or, as a
last resort, water and stock cube
2 tablespoons sherry
1 teaspoon redcurrant jelly

4 large sprigs tarragon
2 heaped teaspoons aspic
4 good tablespoons Hellman's mayonnaise
1 tablespoon chopped fresh or dried tarragon

Serves 4

Bring the stock, sherry and jelly to the boil then pull off the stove. Put in the chicken breasts, lay the sprigs of tarragon on top and cover tightly. Put pan on the merest thread of heat, if possible on a heat-reducing mat, and poach for 20 minutes. The water should barely move. Remove breasts, leave to cool, then refrigerate. Reduce the stock to ¼ pint/150 ml and melt the aspic in it. Strain and cool. When it reaches a syrupy consistency stir into the mayonnaise together with the chopped tarragon. Coat each breast well and lay in a shallow lidded plastic container.

PITTA BREADS

Before you leave home flash the pitta breads under the grill for a minute, then insert a sharp knife down one side and make a pocket. Each person can put his chicken breast inside and munch it in his fingers.

MIXED SALAD

Make a salad of Little Gem lettuce, lollo rosso or radiccio, finely sliced fennel and cherry tomatoes. Tear the leaves up small so that they are easy to eat with a fork. Pack into a lidded plastic box. Take a screwtop jar with Archie's Dressing (see p.15) and mix it into the salad on site.

ICED LEMON AND MINT TEA

Make a pot of weak china tea. Fill a china jug with ice, a bunch of mint leaves, 2 or 3 slices of lemon and a few lumps of sugar. Pour over the tea and then transfer to a well chilled thermos.

TRICK OF THE TRADE Pouring the hot tea over the ice makes a much more delicate drink than using tea which has been allowed to brew and then get cold, which produces a cloudy and unappetising liquid.

MENU
SMOKED SALMON AND AVOCADO MOUSSES
CHICKEN LIVER TERRINE WITH PORT
OYSTER MUSHROOMS À LA GRECQUE WITH GREEN
FLAGEOLET BEANS
HONEYDEW MELON AND RUM
ICED CARDAMOM COFFEE

SMOKED SALMON AND AVOCADO MOUSSES

8 oz/225 g smoked salmon pieces	*½ teaspoon Worcester Sauce*
3 ripe avocados	*1 dessertspoon lemon juice*
¼ pkt Philadelphia cream cheese	*2 spring onions finely chopped*
1 dash tabasco sauce	*4 quail's eggs (optional)*

Serves 4

Purée the smoked salmon, lemon juice, cream cheese and seasonings in the Magimix until really smooth, then add the peeled and stoned avocados. Blend for a few seconds more until smooth then stir in the chopped spring onions. Fill small ramekins right to the brim and cover tightly with cling-film. Refrigerate. Optional: if you like you can press a hard-boiled quail's egg into each pot and smooth over the top.

CHICKEN LIVER TERRINE WITH PORT

1 lb/450 g chicken or turkey livers	4 fl oz/100 ml port
8 oz/225 g ham	1 egg
5 oz/150 g pork sausage meat	Allspice
1 thick slice white bread without crusts, soaked in milk	Salt and ground black pepper
1 dessertspoon chopped parsley	Fat streaky rashers for lining terrine

Serves 4-6

Trim the livers and marinade in the port with salt, pepper and allspice. Chop the ham and mix with the bread, egg, sausage meat and parsley. Line a terrine with the strips of bacon and put in alternate layers of mixture and livers, ending with mixture. Place a couple of bay leaves on top, cover tightly with foil and then the lid. Cook in a pre-heated oven at 400°F/200°C/Gas Mark 6. Place a weight on top and cool, then refrigerate for 2-3 days. Serve in its dish.

OYSTER MUSHROOMS À LA GRECQUE AND GREEN FLAGEOLET BEANS

5 oz/150 g oyster mushrooms	1 dessertspoon parsley, chopped
1 clove garlic, finely chopped	1 tin green flageolet beans
2 tablespoons best cold-pressed olive oil	Salt and ground black pepper
1 dessertspoon lemon juice	

Cut the oyster mushrooms into thin strips and cook over a low heat with the garlic, olive oil and lemon juice for about 5 minutes. Stir and shake constantly. Remove from stove, cover with a lid and leave to get cool. Drain the beans well and add to the mushrooms together with the parsley. Transfer to a lidded plastic container.

HONEYDEW MELON AND RUM

Remove a round of the melon with an apple corer. Pour in some rum and plug up with the melon 'cork'. Wrap tightly in cling-film and refrigerate. Keep upright in fridge and when transporting it.

ICED CARDAMOM COFFEE

Place a crushed cardamom seed, 1 heaped tablespoon Continental-type instant coffee and 1 dessertspoon coffee sugar in a jug. Pour on ½ pint/275 ml boiling water and leave for 10 minutes. Stir and then strain into another jug. Add ice and 1 pint/575 ml milk. Refrigerate and pour into a well-chilled thermos.

MENU
HARD-BOILED EGGS STUFFED WITH PÂTÉ
CÔTELETTES EN CHEMISE
NEW POTATOES AND GREEN PEAS IN
MINT JELLY DRESSING
CLAFOUTI
SANGRIA

HARD-BOILED EGGS STUFFED WITH PÂTÉ

Mix together the yolks of the hard-boiled eggs with liver sausage or pâté, mayonnaise, chopped spring onion, gherkin and parsley. Fill each half and stick together. Allow 2 eggs per person.

CÔTELETTES EN CHEMISE

4-8 lamb cutlets with bones	*1 egg yolk beaten with a little milk*
Redcurrant jelly	*Salt and pepper*
1 tablespoon oil	*Shortcrust pastry (see p.30)*

Serves 4

Trim every scrap of fat off the cutlets and scrape the bones. Heat the oil in a thick pan until it is smoking. Sear the cutlets for 1 minute on each side, remove and cool. Make a shortcrust pastry and roll it out thinly into a long rectangle. Cut into requisite number of strips 1 in/3 cm wide and wet the edges. Salt and pepper the cutlets and wind the pastry round each one in a spiral leaving the bone 'handles' free, and seal the ends. Brush with beaten egg. Bake on a greased baking sheet in a pre-heated oven at 400°F/200°C/Gas Mark 6 for ten minutes then turn down to 350°F/175°C/Gas Mark 4 for a further 10 minutes. Cool and place on kitchen paper in a shallow lidded plastic container.

GREEN PEA AND NEW POTATO SALAD WITH MINT JELLY DRESSING

Cook 1 lb/450 g new potatoes and 1 x 1 lb/450 g pkt frozen petit pois. When cool mix with 1 tablespoon mint jelly, 1 dessertspoon vinegar, salt and pepper.

CLAFOUTI

On my first never-to-be forgotten visit to France my parents, uncle and I were frightened of being benighted, so we stopped at a little hamlet perched up in the Massif Central. There was a tiny hotel and mine host made us most welcome. Madame asked us if we would mind waiting for dinner. I shall never forget it. A meltingly delicate tarte of cream, hard-boiled eggs and wild mushrooms, freshly caught trout from the mountain stream which ran through the hamlet, cooked with wild herbs and butter and, to end with, a local speciality of the Limousin district — Clafouti. Traditionally it is made with cherries, but you can use any kind of fruit and this particular one is made with grapes.

8 oz/225 g plain flour	1 pinch salt
8 oz/225 g caster sugar	4 teaspoons cognac
4 eggs	1 lb/450 g white grapes, de-seeded (muscat
1 pint/575 ml milk	if possible)

Serves 4-6

Sieve the flour, salt and sugar into the Magimix. Heat the milk until it is lukewarm. Switch on the Magimix and break in the eggs one by one and then pour in the milk and cognac. Butter a shallow, ovenproof dish and scatter the grapes over the bottom. Pour on the batter and place in a pre-heated oven at 400°F/200°C/Gas Mark 6 for 25 minutes. Cool and refrigerate. Take along in its dish, cut into wedges or squares and serve with double cream.

SANGRIA

Mix together the juice of 1 lemon and 2 oranges, 1 bottle red wine (Spanish to be authentic), 1 small sherry glass each of brandy and cointreau, sugar to taste and slices of orange and lemon or lime. Add ice and at the last minute on site a 500 ml bottle of soda water, but if you want to make it less potent use more to dilute. Many is the time I have drunk this at shooting lunches in Spain and even more copious quantities of 103 Spanish brandy and cointreau in the evening. I often wondered how the Guns managed to shoot at all the next day.

I hope you have found something helpful in this book. I have tried to include some unusual recipes, both English and Continental. My cry is — be adventurous and try out new things. Even if it seems a bore and a chore, do have some stock in your deep freeze, it makes such a difference to soups and sauces, and don't be afraid to experiment. And last but not least never shun the short cut, no-one will ever know. *Bon appetit!*

INDEX

Entries in **bold** type denote recipes and the page numbers for them.

Anchovy Butter, 10
Ann's Winter Summer Pudding, 52
Apple Cake, Linda's Spiced, 63
Apple Charlotte, 52
Apple Tart, French, 36; shortcrust pastry for, 36
Apricot/Nut Spread, (sandwich), **99**
Archie's Dressing, 15, 26, 84, 109
Archie's Favourite (bap), **18**
Avocado Mousse, Smoked Salmon and, 110

Bacon and Lettuce (sandwich), **19**
Baked Bean, Bacon and Cheese (sandwich), **101**
Baked Smoked Pork Loin with Chutney Sauce, 27
Basic Flavoured Butter, 10
Bean Soup, Florentine, 7
Béchamel sauce, 42, 82
Beef (sandwich), **11**
Beef Roly-Poly, 47
Beurre Manié, 46
Bloody Mary (Archie's explosive), 74, 75
Boiled Chicken and Egg Sauce, 42
Breach Orange Vodka, 92
Bread and Butter Pudding, Cold French, 37
Breast of Pigeon Goodwife, 39
Bubble and Squeak, 50, 51-2
Bullshot, Hot, 90
BUTTERS:
  Anchovy, **10,** 11; Basic Flavoured, **10;** Cumberland, **10;** Curried, **10;** Ravigote, **10;** Tartare, **10**

Cardamon Coffee, Iced, 112
Carrot and Coriander Soup, 23
Carrots, Lucy's Buttered, 35
Cassoulet, 1, 48-50
Celeriac Remoulade, 73, 83
Chanterelles, 3
Chanterelle Soup, 7-8
Chaudfroid of Chicken (pitta), **109**
CHECK LISTS:
  driven grouse shooting, 5; walked-up grouse shooting, 14; driven partridge shooting (September), 21; pheasant shooting (lunch in a shooting hut), 56; pheasant shooting (lunch from a Land-Rover), 65; midsummer pigeon picnic, 107
Cheese and Beer Spread (sandwich), **100**
Cheese Sauce (for **Mince with Lasagne Topping**), **41**
Chicken (sandwich), **11**
Chicken, Boiled, and Egg Sauce, 42; sauce for, 42
Chicken, Chaudfroid of (pitta), **109**

Chicken and Lemon Soup, Fennel, 22
Chicken and Tongue (sandwich), **11**
Chicken Liver Pâté, Grouse and, 11
Chicken Livers, Sautéed, in Crispy Baps, 67
Chicken Liver Terrine with Port, 111
Chicken, Mayonnaise, Almond and Chopped Watercress (bap), **105**
Chicken or Partridge Liver Pâté Paprika, 73, 77
Chicken Salad, 26
Chicken Soup, Curried, 66-7
Chicken Soup, Lucy's American Sweetcorn and, 6
Chicory, Orange and Juniper Salad, 73, 83
Choccy Pots, 73, 85, 85-6
Chocolate Brownies, 15
Chocolate Cake, Sophie's, 31-2
Chocolate Roll (roll), **100**
Citron Pressé, 104, 106
Clafouti, 113-4
Coats, Major A. J., 1, 3, 4, 13, 15, 18, 20, 33, 34, 38, 43, 47, 57, 63, 68, 74-5, 85, 91, 94, 98, 99, 101-2, 104, 106, 108
Coats, Lucy (Mrs J. R. Owen), 1, 4, 6, 25-6, 35, 39, 55, 93, disagreement about **Spanish Omelette,** 25-6; as undergraduate, 35; alleged inability to cook rice, 39
Cold Curried Mince and Chutney (bap), **99**
Cold French Bread and Butter Pudding, 37
Confit d'Oie Sauvage, 49, 50, 59
Consommé, Game, 23-4
Constance, Aunt, 52, 69-70
Constance's Game Patties, 69-70; pastry for, 70
Cooked Salad Dressing, 27
Coriander Soup, Carrot and, 23
Corned Beef and Horseradish with Cream Cheese, Mustard, Parsley and Mayonnaise (sandwich), **105**
Côtelettes en Chemise, 112-3
Cream Cheese and Apple Jelly (sandwich), **99**
Cream Cheese, Jelly and Watercress (roll), **101**
Cream Cheese, Liver Pâté and Crispy Bacon (sandwich), **99**
Cumberland Butter, 10
Cumberland Sauce, 10
Curried Butter, 10
Curried Chicken Soup, 66-7

Date and Honey Bar, Linda's, 71
Date Loaf, 62
Devilled Kidneys, see **'Shootable Stag'**
Dogs, food and drink for, 14, 21, 44, 56, 107
Don, Duncan, 3

DRESSINGS, SALAD, *see* SALADS
  AND DRESSINGS
DRINKS:
  Bloody Mary (Archie's explosive), 74, 75
  Breach Orange Vodka, 92
  Citron Pressé, 104, 106
  drinks, mid-morning, 89; **recipes for, 90-3**
  Hot Bullshot, 90
  Iced Cardamom Coffee, 112
  Iced Lemon and Mint Tea, 109-10
  Lucy's Raspberry Vodka, 93
  Prue's Punch, 90-1
  Ralph's Rum, 94
  Sangria, 114
  Sloe Gin, 91
  Tom's Tipple, 94
Duck Liver Pâté with Brandy and Truffles, 73, 75-6
Duck, magret of, 49
Duck (Wild), Salmi of Oxtail and, 44-5, *see also*
  Oxtail Stew
Dumplings, Herby (for **Ray's Mince and Herby**
  Dumplings), 48

EGGS:
  Egg Sauce (for **Boiled Chicken and Egg Sauce**), 42
  Gladys's Scotch Eggs, 68
  Hard-Boiled Eggs Stuffed with Pâté, 112
  Spanish Omelette, 25-6
  Stuffed Egg, 99
Egg Sauce (for **Boiled Chicken and Egg Sauce**), 42
Egg, Stuffed, 99
Elderberry Mousse, 73, 86

Fennel, Chicken and Lemon Soup, 22
Fennel in Pernod Sauce, 73, 84
Feta Cheese, Olives and Tomatoes (baguette), **105**
Filled Pitta Breads, 68
FISH:
  Fish pie, 1
  Peta's Tuna Fish Salad, 24
  Smoked Salmon and Avocado Mousse, 110
  Smoked Salmon Pâté, 12
  Smoked Trout Pâté, 11
  Smoked Trout Pâté with Almonds, 73, 79
  See also **SANDWICHES, BAGUETTES, BAPS,**
  FILLED PITTA BREADS
Florentine Bean Soup, 7
Four O'Clock Feast, The (pheasant shooting), 1, 43,
  72-5; menu for, 73; **recipes for, 75-88;** planning for,
  74-5; mid-morning snacks and drinks before, 89-90;
  recipes for snacks and drinks, 90-3. *See also* PHEA-
  SANT SHOOTING: lunch at home.
French Apple Tart, 36; shortcrust pastry for, 36

French Bread and Butter Pudding, Cold, 37
Fruit Cake, Tania's Boil and Bake, 62

Galantine, Pork, 28-9
Galette, Potato, 28
GAME AND POULTRY:
  Boiled Chicken and Egg Sauce, 42
  Breast of Pigeon Goodwife, 39
  Cassoulet, 1, 48-50
  Chaudfroid of Chicken, 109
  Chicken Salad, 26
  Confit d'Oie Sauvage, 49, 50, 59
  Constance's Game Patties, 69-70; pastry for, 70
  Game Consommé, 23-4
  Grouse Soup, 8
  Magret of duck, 49
  Romany Soup, 61
  Salmi of Oxtail and Wild Duck, 44-5; *see also*
    Oxtail Stew,
  Venison Stew, 46
  Venison Stock, 46
  See also **MEAT; PÂTÉS, TERRINES, PIES;**
    SANDWICHES, BAGUETTES,
    BAPS, FILLED PITTA BREADS
Game Conservancy Trust, The, 5
Game Consommé, 23-4
Game Patties, Constance's, 69-70; pastry for, 70
Garbure, 59
Garfit, Will, 74-5, 89
Gingerbread, Jenny Gay's, 100-1
Gin, Sloe, 91
Gladys's Scotch Eggs, 68
Goulash Soup, 59-60
Green Pea and New Potato Salad with Mint Jelly
  Dressing, 113
Grouse (sandwich), **11**
Grouse and Chicken Liver Pâté (sandwich), **11**
Grouse Pâté with Whisky and Juniper Berries, 73,
  76-7
Grouse Soup, 8
GROUSE SHOOTING:
  driven, 3-4; **recipes for, 6-12, 29**
  walked-up, 12-13; **recipes for, 13-14**
Gullick, Tom, 3, 4, 20, 24, 25, 38, 55, 74-5, 90, 101
Gullick, Mary, 4

Ham (sandwich), **11**
Ham, Emmental, Tomato and Spring Onion (pitta),
  99
Ham in Parsley Sauce Gratiné, 42; sauce for, 42
Hard-Boiled Eggs Stuffed with Pâté, 112
Hauxton, shoot at, 89

Herby Dumplings (for **Ray's Mince and Herby Dumplings**), 48
Honeydew Melon and Rum, 112
Hot Bullshot, 90
Hunter's Sandwich, 18

Iced Cardamom Coffee, 112
Iced Lemon and Mint Tea, 109-10
Ishimael's Peanut Butter Soup, 103
Jam or Treacle Layer Pudding, 53-4; suet pastry for, 54
Jenny Gay's Gingerbread, 100-1

Kidneys (Lamb's), Devilled, *see* 'Shootable Stag'
Kissel, 53

Lamb en Daube, 40-1; marinade for, 40
Land-Rover (and other 4WD vehicles), 3, 20, 104
  lunch from, 64-5; **recipes for, 65-71**
Lasagne Topping, Mince with, 41; Cheese Sauce for, 41
Lemon and Mint Tea, Iced, 109-10
Lettuce Salad, Radiccio and, 73, 84
Linda's Date and Honey Bar, 71
Linda's Spiced Apple Cake, 63
Lucy's American Sweetcorn and Chicken Soup, 6
Lucy's Buttered Carrots, 35
Lucy's Raspberry Vodka, 93
Lunch boxes (for pigeon shooting); **recipes for, 99-101, 105-6**

Magret of duck, 49
Main Course Minestrone, 57-8
Mallard with Madeira and Orange, Terrine of, 73, 81
Marinade for **Lamb en Daube**, 40
MEAT:
  Baked Smoked Pork Loin with Chutney Sauce, 27
  Beef Roly-Poly, 47
  Côtelettes en Chemise, 112-3
  Ham in Parsley Sauce Gratiné, 42: sauce for, 42
  Lamb en Daube, 40-1
  Mince with Lasagne Topping, 41; Cheese Sauce for, 41
  Oxtail Stew, 73, 85; *see also* Salmi of Oxtail and Wild Duck
  Ray's Mince and Herby Dumplings, 47-8
  Savoury Sausageburgers, 18
  'Shootable Stag' (Devilled Kidneys), 73, 85
  Toad in the Hole, 50-1
  Veal or Pork Casserole with Apples, Onions, Cider and Calvados, 35-6
  See also **GAME AND POULTRY; PÂTÉS, TERRINES, PIES; SANDWICHES, BAGUETTES, BAPS, FILLED PITTA BREADS**

Melon and Rum, Honeydew, 112
Mince and Herby Dumplings, Ray's, 47-8
Mince with Lasagne Topping, 41; Cheese Sauce for, 41
Minestrone, Main Course, 57-8
Mulligatawny soup, 66; *see also* **Curried Chicken Soup**
Mushrooms à la Grecque, 24-5
Mushrooms (Oyster) à la Grecque and Green Flageolet Beans, 111
Nannie's Soda Scones, 16
Niçoise, Simple Salade, 26
Nut Spread, *see* Apricot/Nut Spread
Omelette, Spanish, 25-6
Onion and Mustard (sandwich), 100
Orange Vodka, Breach, 92
Owen, J. Richard ('Piggy'), 39, 52
Oxtail and Wild Duck, Salmi of, 44-5; *see also* **Oxtail Stew**
Oxtail Soup, 65-6; 'quick cheat' for, 66
Oxtail Stew, 73, 85; *see also* **Salmi of Oxtail and Wild Duck**
Oyster Mushrooms à la Grecque and Green Flageolet Beans, 111

Parsley Sauce (for **Ham in Parsley Sauce Gratiné**), 42
PARTRIDGE SHOOTING:
  driven, 20-1, 33, 38; **recipes for, 22-32, 33-7, 39-42**
  in France, 20
  in Spain, 3, 20-1, 24, 25, 38, 47, 55-6, 94, 114
Partridge (or Chicken) Liver Pâté Paprika, 73, 77
Pastry, Samosa, 69
Pastry, Shortcrust: for **Pork and Apple Pie**, 30; for French Apple Tart, 36
Pastry, Suet (for **Jam or Treacle Layer Pudding**), 54
PÂTÉS, TERRINES, PIES:
  Chicken Liver Terrine with Port, 111
  Duck Liver Pâté with Brandy and Truffles, 73, 75-6
  Fish pie, 1
  Grouse Pâté with Whisky and Juniper Berries, 73, 76-7
  Partridge (or Chicken) Liver Pâté Paprika, 73, 77
  Pigeon Pie, 33-4
  Pork and Apple Pie, 30; shortcrust pastry for, 30
  Pork Galantine, 28-9
  Smoked Pigeon Pâté with Vermouth and Honey, 73, 78
  Smoked Salmon Pâté, 12
  Smoked Trout Pâté, 11
  Smoked Trout Pâté with Almonds, 73, 79
  Terrine of Mallard with Madeira and Orange, 73, 81
  Terrine of Pigeon with Sloe Gin, 73, 79-80

Veal Pâté en Croute, 29
See also GAME AND POULTRY; MEAT; SAND-
WICHES, BAGUETTES, BAPS, FILLED
PITTA BREADS
Peanut Butter, Carrot, Bacon and Mayonnaise
(sandwich), 100
Peanut Butter, Carrot, Raisins, and Orange Juice
(sandwich), 100
Peanut Butter Soup, Ishimael's, 99–100, 103
Pea (Split) Soup with Pork, Scandinavian Yellow,
57
Peta's Tuna Fish Salad, 24
PHEASANT SHOOTING:
October and November, lunch at home, 43–4, 72, 85;
'forward thinking' for, 43–4; **recipes for, 44–54**
lunch in a shooting hut, 55–6; **recipes for, 57–63**
lunch from a Land-Rover, 64–5; **recipes for, 65–71;**
see also **SHOOTING-STICK FOOD AND
OTHER SNACKS**
Four O'Clock Feast, The, 72–5; menu for, 73; **recipes
for, 76–88;** *See also* PHEASANT SHOOTING: lunch
at home, mid-morning snacks and drinks before The
Four O'Clock Feast, 89–90; **recipes for drinks, 90–3**
Pigeon Goodwife, Breast of, 39
Pigeon Pâté with Vermouth and Honey, Smoked,
73, 78
Pigeon Pie, 33–4
Pigeon with Sloe Gin, Terrine of, 73, 79–80
PIGEON SHOOTING:
winter, 98; lunch boxes for, 99–101; **recipes for,
99–103;** summer, 104, 106, 101, 112; lunch boxes for
105–6 **recipes for, 105–6, 108–14**
'Piggy', *see* Owen, J. Richard
Pork and Apple Pie, 30; shortcrust pastry for, 30
Pork Galantine, 28–9
Pork Loin with Chutney Sauce, Baked Smoked, 27
Pork or Veal Casserole with Apples, Onions, Cider
and Calvados, 35–6
Potato Galette, 28
Prawns, Chopped Fennel and Mayonnaise (bap), 105
Prue's Perfect Rice, 39–40, 85
Prue's Punch, 90–1
PUDDINGS, CAKES, SWEET SNACKS, ETC.
Ann's Winter Summer Pudding, 52
Apple Charlotte, 52
Apricot/Nut Spread (sandwich), 99
Choccy Pots, 73, 85, 85–6
Chocolate Brownies, 15
Chocolate Roll (roll), 100
Clafouti, 113–4
Cold French Bread and Butter Pudding, 37
Date Loaf, 62
Elderberry Mousse, 73, 86

French Apple Tart, 36; shortcrust pastry for, 36
Honeydew Melon and Rum, 112
Jam or Treacle Layer Pudding, 53–4; suet pastry
for, 54
Jenny Gay's Gingerbread, 100–1
Kissel, 53
Linda's Spiced Apple Cake, 63
Linda's Date and Honey Bar, 71
Nannie's Soda Scones, 16
Rich Creamy Rice Pudding, 53
Rumpot, fruit from, 31
Shortcrust Pastry, (for French Apple Tart), 36
Sophie's Chocolate Cake, 31–2
Suet Pastry (for Jam or Treacle Layer Pudding), 54
Summer Pudding with a Difference, 31
Tangerine Sorbet, 73, 87–8
Tania's Boil and Bake Fruit Cake, 62
Pumpkin and Tomato Soup, 101–2
Punch, Prue's, 90–1

Quiche Lorraine, flabbiness of, 1; author once enjoyed, 3

Radiccio and Lettuce Salad, 73, 84
Ralph's Rum, 94
Raspberry Vodka, Lucy's, 93
Ravigote Butter, 10
Ray's Mince and Herby Dumplings, 47–8
Remoulade, Celeriac, 83
Rich Creamy Rice Pudding, 53
Rice, Prue's Perfect, 39–40, 85
Rice Pudding, Rich Creamy, 53
Roly-Poly, Beef, 47
Romany Soup, 61
Rum, Ralph's, 94
Rumpot, fruit from, 31

SALADS AND DRESSINGS:
Archie's Dressing, 15, 26, 84, 109
Celeriac Remoulade, 73, 83
Chicken Salad, 26
Chicory, Orange and Juniper Salad, 73, 83
Cooked Salad Dressing, 27
Fennel in Pernod Sauce, 73, 84
Green Pea and New Potato Salad with Mint Jelly
Dressing, 113
Mixed salad, 109
Mushrooms à la Grecque, 24–5
Oyster Mushrooms à la Grecque and Green
Flageolet Beans, 111
Peta's Tuna Fish Salad, 24
Radiccio and Lettuce Salad, 73, 84
Simple Salade Niçoise, 26
Tomato and Basil Salad, 25

Tomato Ring, 73, 84
Salad, mixed, 109
Salade Niçoise, Simple, 26
Salmi of Oxtail and Wild Duck, 44–5; *see also* Oxtail Stew
Salmon (Smoked) and Avocado Mousse, 110
Salmon Pâté, Smoked, 12
Samosas, 69; pastry for, 69
SANDWICHES, BAGUETTES, BAPS, FILLED PITTA BREADS:
  Apricot/Nut Spread, 99
  Archie's Favourite, 18
  Bacon and Lettuce, 19
  Baked Bean, Bacon and Cheese, 101
  Beef, 11
  Chaudfroid of Chicken, 109
  Cheese and Beer Spread, 100
  Chicken, 11
  Chicken and Tongue, 11
  Chicken, Mayonnaise, Almond and Chopped Watercress, 105
  Chocolate Roll, 100
  Cold Curried Mince and Chutney, 99
  Corned Beef and Horseradish with Cream Cheese, Mustard, Parsley and Mayonnaise, 105
  Cream Cheese and Apple Jelly, 99
  Cream Cheese, Jelly and Watercress, 101
  Cream Cheese, Liver Pâté and Crispy Bacon, 99
  Feta Cheese, Olives and Tomatoes, 105
  Filled Pitta Breads, 68
  Grouse, 11
  Grouse and Chicken Liver Pâté, 11
  Ham, 11
  Ham, Emmental, Tomato and Spring Onion, 99
  Hunter's Sandwich, 18
  Onion and Mustard, 100
  Peanut Butter, Carrot, Bacon and Mayonnaise, 100
  Peanut Butter, Carrot, Raisins and Orange Juice, 100
  Prawns, Chopped Fennel and Mayonnaise, 105
  Sardine Special, 99
  Sautéed Chicken Livers in Crispy Baps, 67
  Shredded Cabbage, Carrot, Spring Onion, Ham and Mayonnaise, 105
  Smoked Trout, Hard-Boiled Egg, Fromage Frais and Dill Butter, 106
  Smoked Salmon Pâté, 12
  Smoked Trout Pâté, 11
  Tuna, 11
Sangria, 114
Sardine Special (bap), 99

SAUCES:
  Béchamel, 42, 82
  Beurre Manié, 46
  Cheese (for Mince with Lasagne Topping), 41
  Cumberland, 10
  Egg (for Boiled Chicken and Egg Sauce), 42
  Parsley (for Ham in Parsley Sauce Gratiné), 42
Sausageburgers, Savoury, 18
Sausage Parcel, 67
Sautéed Chicken Livers in Crispy Baps, 67
Savoury Sausageburgers, 18
Scandinavian Yellow Split Pea Soup with Pork, 57
Scones, Nannie's Soda, 16
Scotch Eggs, Gladys's, 68
'Shootable Stag' (Devilled Kidneys), 73, 85
SHOOTING-STICK FOOD AND OTHER SNACKS:
  Constance's Game Patties, 69–70; pastry for, 70
  Filled Pitta Breads, 68
  Gladys's Scotch Eggs, 68
  Linda's Date and Honey Bar, 71
  Linda's Spiced Apple Cake, 63
  Nannie's Soda Scones, 16
  Samosas, 69; pastry for, 69
  Sausage Parcel, 67
  Sautéed Chicken Livers in Crispy Baps, 67
  Shooting-stick food, 67–71
  Snacks and drinks, mid-morning, 89–93

SHOOT LUNCHES: ideas for, different types of, requirements of, 1, 2, 3–4, 13, 17, 20, 33, 38, 43–4, 55–6, 64–5, 72–5, 89–90, 94–5, 97, 98, 99, 104, 106, 108, 114; *see also* GROUSE SHOOTING; PARTRIDGE SHOOTING; PHEASANT SHOOTING; PIGEON SHOOTING; STALKING; WILDFOWLING.
Shortcrust Pastry; for Pork and Apple Pie, 30; for Pigeon Pie, 34; for French Apple Tart, 36; for Côtelettes en Chemise, 113
Shredded Cabbage, Carrot, Spring Onion, Ham and Mayonnaise (pitta), 105
Simple Salade Niçoise, 26
Sloe Gin, 91
Smoked Pigeon Pâté with Vermouth and Honey, 73, 78
Smoked Salmon and Avocado Mousse, 110
Smoked Salmon Pâté (sandwich), 12
Smoked Trout, Hard-Boiled Egg, Fromage Frais and Dill Butter (sandwich), 106
Smoked Trout Pâté, 11
Smoked Trout Pâté with Almonds, 73, 79

SNACKS: *see* **SHOOTING-STICK FOOD AND OTHER SNACKS**

Snacks and drinks, mid-morning (pheasant shooting), 89–90; **recipes for drinks, 90–3.** *See also* **SHOOTING-STICK FOOD AND OTHER SNACKS**

Soda Scones, Nannie's, 16

Sophie's Chocolate Cake, 31–2

Sophy (the redoubtable), 47, 69

Sorbet, Tangerine, 73, **87–8**

Sorrel soup, 4

Sorrel Soup, Spinach and, 108

SOUPS, STOCK:

   Carrot and Coriander, 23

   Chanterelle, 7–8

   Curried Chicken, 66–7

   Fennel, Chicken and Lemon, 22

   Florentine Bean, 7

   Game Consommé, 23–4

   Garbure, 59

   Goulash Soup, 59–60

   Grouse, 8

   Ishimael's Peanut Butter, 103

   Lucy's American Sweetcorn and Chicken, 6

   Main Course Minestrone, 57–8

   Mulligatawny, 66; *see also* **Curried Chicken Soup**

   Oxtail, 65–6; 'quick cheat' for, 66

   Pumpkin and Tomato, 101–2

   Romany, 61

   Scandinavian Yellow Split Pea with Pork, 57

   Sorrel soup, 4

   Soups, mid-morning before Four O'Clock Feast, 90

   Spinach and Sorrel, 108

   Swede, 4, 6

   Venison stock, 46

Spanish Omelette, 25–6

Spiced Apple Cake, Linda's, 63

Spinach Mousse with Cheese and Hard-Boiled Egg, 73, **82**

Spinach and Sorrel Soup, 108

Split Pea Soup, Scandinavian Yellow, 57

STALKING, 17; **recipes for, 18–19**

Stew, Venison, 46

Stuffed Egg, 99

Suet Pastry (for Jam or Treacle Layer Pudding), 54

Summer Pudding, Ann's Winter, 52

Summer Pudding with a Difference, 31

Swede Soup, 4, 6

Sweetcorn and Chicken Soup, Lucy's American, 6

Tangerine Sorbet, 73, **87–8**

Tania's Boil and Bake Fruit Cake, 62

Tartare Butter, 10

Terrine of Mallard with Madeira and Orange, 73, **81**

Terrine of Pigeon with Sloe Gin, 73, **79–80**

Toad in the Hole, 50–1

Tomato and Basil Salad, 25

Tomato Ring, 73, **84**

Tomato Soup, Pumpkin and, 101–2

Tom's Tipple, 94

Tower Hill, shoot at, 1, 44, 72–5, 91; menu for, 73

Treacle or Jam Layer Pudding, 53–4; **suet pastry for, 54**

TRICKS OF THE TRADE:

   soup, 8; baps, 14; Mars Bars for dogs, 14; keeping bread warm outdoors, 30; serving **Summer Pudding,** 31; removing fat from stock, soups, or casseroles, 45; thickening beef stews with oxtail soup, 45; 'quick cheat' for **Oxtail Soup,** 66; iced tea, 110

Trout Pâté, Smoked (sandwich), **11**

Trout (Smoked) Pâté with Almonds, 73, **79**

Tuna (sandwich), **11**

Tuna Fish Salad, Peta's, 24

Veal or Pork Casserole with Apples, Onions, Cider and Calvados, 35–6

Veal Pâté en Croute, 29

VEGETABLES AND OTHER ACCOMPANIMENTS:

   Bubble and Squeak, 50, **51–52**

   Herby Dumplings (for **Ray's Mince and Herby Dumplings**), 48

   Lucy's Buttered Carrots, 35

   Potato Galette, 28

   Prue's Perfect Rice, 39–40, 85

   Smoked Salmon and Avocado Mousse, 110

   Spinach Mousse with Cheese and Hard-Boiled Egg, 73, **82**

Tomato Ring, 73, **84**

See also **SALADS AND DRESSINGS**

Venison Stew, 46

Venison Stock, 46

Vodka, Breach Orange, 92

Vodka, Lucy's Raspberry, 93

Wildfowler's Brunch or High Tea, menus for, 95–6

WILDFOWLING, 94–5; **recipes for, 94–7**

Woodmarsh, shoot at, 63